For Bob

Elvis may be dead, but Kwelvis — the Key West
version of Elvis — is alive and well, living it up in paradise.
Have you had a Kwelvis sighting?

FROM THE AUTHORS OF QUIT YOUR JOB AND MOVE TO KEY WEST

KEY WEST 101

Discovering Paradise

Warning:
Contains laid back
themes and margarita
induced humor!

Christopher
SHULTZ

David
SLOAN

KEY WEST 101

Discovering Paradise

Christopher Shultz   David L. Sloan

PHANTOM PRESS
KEY WEST, FLORIDA

Phantom Press
P.O. Box 4766
Key West, FL 33041
www.phantompress.com

Cover design: Peter Downie @ Wodumedia.com
Layout and design: Kerry Karshna
Photos: Rob O'Neal
Editing: Mandy Bolen
Carl the crazy conch design: Jodi Bombace
Beer: None on this one

10 9 8 7 6 5 4 3 2 1st edition worth lots of money on e-bay!
Buy two copies.
ISBN# 0-9674498-6-3

KEY WEST 101
Discovering Paradise

Christopher Shultz   David L. Sloan

PHANTOM PRESS
KEY WEST, FLORIDA

It's A Living Thing

1. People
2. Key Deer
3. Tourists
4. Chickens
5. Conchs
6. Pirates
7. Dogs
8. Drag Queens
9. Military
10. Celebrities
11. Locals
12. Cats
13. Street Musicians
14. Birds
15. Key West Characters
16. Geckos
17. Chris and David

What's The Function?

18. 2x4 Mile Island
19. Flora and Fauna
20. Parks
21. Salt Ponds
22. Sunrise
23. Sunset
24. Climate
25. Beaches
26. Duval Street
27. Hidden Lanes
28. Bahama Village
29. Hurricanes
30. Tropical Breezes
31. Infrastructure
32. Airport
33. Homes
34. Architecture
35. Cuba
36. Stock Island
37. History
38. Big Cities
39. Secret Spots
40. Conch Republic
41. Location
42. Mile Markers
43. Jobs
44. Cruise Ships

Hot Fun In The Summer Time

45. Drinks
46. Stars
47. Sports
48. Outer Islands
49. Fitness
50. Art
51. Music
52. Festivals
53. Attractions
54. Tours
55. Spring Break
56. Fantasy Fest
57. Organizations
58. Sea Life
59. Bars
60. Restaurants
61. Food
62. Cemeteries

63. Churches
64. The Wharf
65. Treasure
66. Scooters
67. Crazy Cars
68. Walkability
69. Fishing
70. Water Sports
71. Reef
72. Lobster Season
73. Sailing
74. Boat Races
75. Margaritaville
76. Mystery
77. Bicycles
79. Small Town Charm
78. Southernmost Point

Off The Deep End

80. Dress Code
81. Tolerance
82. Humor
83. Diversity
84. Opportunity
85. Uniqueness
86. Friendships
87. Adventure
88. Local News
89. Coconut Telegraph
90. Bubba System
91. Funny Signs

92. Self Expression
93. Sounds
94. Community Spirit
95. Attitude
96. Local Radio
97. Smells
98. The Dark Side
99. Citizen's Voice
100. Nicknames
101. Legends
102. You

Discovering
Paradise

photo: RobONeal.com

3

Our last royalty check seemed best spent at the Schooner Wharf Bar. "Quit Your Job and Move to Key West" was a local bestseller, and we were starting to get used to people recognizing us in public. We had barely finished our fifth round when a fellow drunk with four days of stubble, conch chowder stains on an otherwise white shirt and a trucker hat approached with a copy of our book in his hand. "Billy the Mad Cap" was scrawled across the hat in black magic marker.

"Are you the guys who wrote 'Quit Your Job and Move to Key West?'" he asked, slugging back the last of his Miller Lite and gesturing slightly to the book in hand. We were used to the occasional request for an autograph and gave the standard reply.

"That's us, can we sign your copy for you?"

"Screw that! You guys is full of crap."

This was not the response we anticipated. Billy continued, slurring tales of a friend back in Ohio who gave him our book and encouraged him to make the move. As the story went on we became certain that the gift giver was not a friend, but a representative from the City of Dayton nominated to get The Mad Cap out of town for good. The city council was probably sipping martinis as they discussed how many elephants should be brought in for the "Billy is Gone Parade" while we were held captive listening to a tale of woe accompanied by a steady flow of spittle from Billy's mouth. His complaints were valid. Billy dreamed of living in paradise but ended up in hell through a series of unfortunate events. Though we did not feel personally responsible for his misfortunes, the question he kept repeating stuck with us like the spittle that spewed from his mouth every time he said a word starting with the letter 'p': "What is paradise?"

It kept us up at night: The ever present question, "What is paradise?" We stopped drinking and slumped into a great depression trying to find the answer to a question we couldn't quite grasp: the elusive paradise. Is it palm trees blowing in the breeze? Ice cold Coronas from the comfort of a hammock? A "babes vs. hunks" volleyball game on a Tuesday afternoon? They all sound pretty darn good, apart from the hunks, but is this what makes Key West paradise?

Bored, curious and bothered, we decided to do some research to find out what paradise is all about, and what better place to start than the Internet. After several hours getting great deals on Viagra and not looking at porn, we discovered that the word "paradise" originated from the term "pairidaeza," which describes a wall enclosing a garden or orchard. Persian kings and noble men took great pride in maintaining their own gardens and the practice was noted in history books by a Greek mercenary named Xenophon. He described the gardens and the walls with the slightly bastardized "paradeisos," which was taken for use in the bible to describe the Garden of Eden. The word continued its evolution, and today paradise denotes tropical vacation spots across the globe, easily identified by their exotic animals, lush greenery and overpriced frozen drinks.

Paradise was ours - at least by definition, but we still had that empty feeling inside. Isn't there more to paradise than nice weather, coconut palms and a couple of naked people running around? Why do we live in Key West? What makes this place paradise? Why do millions of people come here every year? The questions wouldn't stop, so we turned off the computer, grabbed a couple of Coronas, slipped on our sandals and went looking for answers to the questions that bothered us so.

Key West 101 is a collection of what we discovered; 101 things that make Key West such an incredibly special place; things we found that make this our paradise. Some of the reasons are obvious and some are obscure. A few of them are downright stupid, but who would buy a book called Key West 97? All of them, you will find, are key ingredients in this big pot of southernmost soup we call paradise. Try a bowl yourself. We think you will like it. If not, spill some on your shirt, scrawl your name on a trucker hat and head on down to the Schooner Wharf. We'll give you an autograph.

It's a Living Thing!

photo: RobONeal.com

 # People

Ask any local what they like most about living in Key West and four out of five will tell you it is the people. The person who did not give that answer is into a bizarre type of kinky sex that can only be found in Key West, but "people" is second on his list. When making paradise soup, people are the main ingredient and Key West has such a wide variety even John Lennon didn't imagine them. We are a melting pot of nationalities, colors (including silver), religions, beliefs, and occupations, and though the same could be said for many cities, in Key West no one bats a pupil when they see a gay-Cuban-Methodist cop enjoying a warm cup of coffee with a retired Czech Satanist yoga instructor. Newcomers may think it a strange scene, but anybody who has been here a while will probably just wonder why the yoga instructor left his three-legged ferret at home. There are those who come to Key West and never notice our diverse people. We call them spring breakers.

Local Advice

Wanna hang with the locals? Con leche from
Five Brothers, a glass of wine at Grand Vin, some sun at
Fort Zach and a root beer barrel from the Green Parrot
will give you a healthy dose of local color.
Finish it off with a night cap at La Te Da if you are feeling frisky.

Key Deer

This is a midget-sized deer that, like our little sisters, is super cute and extremely protected. They are the ones to blame for the single lanes and the 35 mph speed limits in Big Pine (the deer, not our sisters), but boy are they cute. If this were a classroom we would bring in a guest speaker from the National Key Deer Refuge. As an alternative we will provide some limited information that may or may not be true, but sounds pretty good and will suffice to amaze your friends who do not check their facts. The Key deer come from your same species as the average North American deer and have identical genetic structures. Their small size is caused largely by the available diet in the Keys (Atkins, Slimfast or cocaine) causing their bodies to adapt to the environment. Another adaptation of the Key deer is their ability to drink salt water. This ability has also been demonstrated by novice snorkelers though there is no known connection between them and the deer. It is a common misconception that the Key deer have poor vision. The truth is that they fail to move for speeding cars, not because they are blinded, but because they are hoping you will stop and offer them a pork rind. In all seriousness, stay away from the deer. If you try to feed them it will draw them out to the road and you will have the death of countless furry animals weighing on your conscience. Stay away from the deer. And stop looking at our sisters.

Frankly, My Deer

Neotoma Floridana Smalli are the smallest deer in United States. They remain pregnant for 204 days and bite when midgets try to ride them.

Tourists

Vacation destinations as a whole deem tourists to be poor tipping, mannerless, resource-raping morons and have adopted an attitude of "give us your money and get the hell out." Key West is different.

Don't get us wrong, we think a few tourists can be poor tipping mannerless, resource-raping morons who should give us their money, but out of the three million people who come here every year most are good in our books. They are easygoing people who are looking to do nothing more than blow off a little steam and get a taste of paradise. Tourists should hang out with the locals. We like drinking with them and they make us feel good about ourselves in one of those strange "watching Jerry Springer" ways. Tourists are such a vital part of our paradise that we would be foolish to do anything but wash their feet, (if they are into that kind of thing) and worship the ground they walk on. They spend a load of money and it keeps the island's economy afloat. You will find that most tourists have a tolerance for the margaritas at Hog's Breath so low they think the hat they just made out of a beer coaster is the best thing since sliced bread.

Two margaritas at Hog's Breath: $8. Cost of Chris and David's drinks over a two-hour conversation: $186. Watching a tourist doing the Macarana with a beer coaster on their head…priceless.

Carl the Crazy Conch says:

Key West has 3,000,000 visitors every year and only 26,000 residents. If the locals were flesh-eating zombies they could each eat 120 people a year without affecting the local population.

4 Chickens

The plight of the Key West chicken; People love them or hate them based solely on the animal's proximity to their bedroom window. This is a sore spot with many locals, but to us it's one of those little tidbits that make Key West such a great place. Is there another city in the world that actually has a chicken festival, a chicken store, and pays somebody to be a chicken wrangler? There are a couple thousand chickens running around Key West originating, some say, from the old cockfighting days or possibly when they were a staple in our diet. The staples kept cutting our stomachs so we switched to paper clips, but the chickens remain.

It doesn't take much to confuse the locals or the chickens in town and it seems the streetlights hate us all. Every night, just after bedtime, they start turning themselves on and off. The chickens think it is sunrise and start their morning crowing routine. The locals think the chickens should be treated to a slow and painful death like the three-day hangover they are suffering, the street lights just think the whole situation is funny (If street lights could think.) Some say, "Damn the chickens!" But how can you stay mad at an animal with such adorable babies who tastes so delicious with two pieces of bacon and a slice of melted cheese? They make us giggle, provide great photo opportunities and give us a great excuse to say cock or breasts in front of our parents. Cock-a-doodle cool!

Over Easy

A chicken and an egg were in bed together having a grand old time. The egg grunted, rolled over and lit up the cigarette, finally answering the age old question as to which came first.

11

Conchs

The mere mention of this friendly mollusk brings smiles to most faces. The smile is usually followed by a laugh because people seem to have one hell of a time pronouncing Conch correctly. The conchs we're talking about don't come from the water, though. They are the true blue people born in Key West. Still confused? Well if you are not one now, give it up because it ain't gonna happen. The closest you can come is drifting off into dreamland on Smathers Beach. When you wake up from your nap, keep your eyes closed for a moment and listen to the sounds. Don't open them yet, we're still taking pictures of you in your bikini. Now open your eyes. This is what the Conchs hear, see and smell when they are born. Conchs are people born in Key West.

Legend has it that the term "conch" evolved from the shell a local doctor would place on a stick in his front yard to announce the birth of a child. Neighbors walking by would see the shell and comment, "Oh, look. He had another Conch." Conchs are the inner fiber of this island and you would be challenged to find more salt of the earth, community-driven folks. They love the island, its history and tradition, as well as the fact that the doctor put a shell on the stick instead of a shoe. Who would want to visit an island with a bunch of high heels running around?

Carl the Crazy Conch Says:

It's bad enough that you grind us up for fritters and douse us with habanero peppers, but putting our shell on a stick is the last straw!

6 Pirates

The term "pirate" may come from the French term *pirratte* meaning conqueror, but it probably doesn't because we just made that up. Remember, we are professors of paradise and like most of America, could care less about anything French. The history of pirates in Key West is muddy at best. Most of the stories are legends told over drinks in the pubs, passed down through the generations or merely made up on the spot in an effort to impress the pretty tourist girls. There may be more pirates on the island today than in all of history combined, but it is tough to tell because the island is full of grown men with earrings and birds on their shoulders looking for a bottle of rum. No matter, pirate stories exist and the island is rife with tales of sunken ships, buried treasure and pirate ghosts that roam the streets at night. So enamored we are with our buccaneer brethren that every year the pirate people of the world congregate in Key West to celebrate what it is to be a pirate. There is no pillaging or raping to be heard of but there is much to be said for drinking, arrgh maties, sailing and swashbuckling. Apart from the occasional sea hag lurking about, this is one of the best festivals in Key West. You can mock them or join them. All they really want are a few ho's and a bottle of rum.

Local Advice

A visit to the Mel Fisher Maritime History Museum or the Pirate Soul Museum owned by Pat Croce of 76er's fame will fill you up with enough pirate knowledge to last a lifetime. No need to hide your wooden leg here.

Dogs

• •

Did you hear about the dyslexic, agnostic, insomniac philosopher? She laid awake all night wondering if there really was a dog.

Key West is for the dogs, which makes Cayo Hueso a pretty cool place. You see them everywhere; walking their human down the street, playing with their chicken neighbors on the sidewalk, sprawled across the floor of the local watering hole with a bowl of suds or even waiting in line at the post office. A dog's personality fits in well down here. They don't like to do much but eat and sleep and play, they don't have any real agenda, and they have a tendency to go around sniffing each other's butts. Sounds like some locals we know.

Anybody who has a dog knows they are like a member of the family, and nothing beats living in a city where the restaurants, bars, stores and boutiques welcome every member of your family – even the one who can't seem to stop licking his privates. Uncle Jimmy and his public antics aside, these places will let you bring your dog in, too. If you don't have a dog of your own, try to borrow one from a local, or just ask the street kids if you can have theirs when it stops being a cute, sympathy-attracting puppy. Dogs are a great way to start conversations with strangers and if you are single and looking they are a sure fire way to get you in practice with your doggy style.

You Can Talk Like Snoop Dogg

Fir Shizzle = For Sure.
Sun Sizzle Celebizzle in da Key Wizzle =
Sunset Celebration in Key West.
Your Dizzle did a Shizzle on my Fizzle =
Your dog just pooped on my foot.

8 Drag Queens

There is something to be said for living in a day and age when the term for a gay man who likes to dress as a woman is easily confused with a beauty pageant winner at the race track. Just working up enough speed to qualify would be tough in Key West, so gentlemen, stop your engines and put on your dancing heels. Nothing puts a smile on your face like a group of drag queens jiggling across Duval Street luring you to their show, with the exception of actually going to the show and letting loose a bit. It's all in good fun, and just like in NASCAR, safety precautions are taken so no one gets hurt. Drag shows have been going on in Key West for decades and they teach us that it is okay to be yourself even if it means wearing a woman's size 16. Let loose and let go! Enjoy a source of entertainment that most people never get to see in the South, where the pit stops are in the bathroom and the crashes come from drunken men in heels hitting the floor. If you feel like drinking your cosmopolitan, pinky raised in the air without the fear of persecution, head upstairs at the 801 or down to LaTe Da. You will be mesmerized by the finest beauty, talent, singing and dancing this side of the speedway broom closet, as well as some darn nice legs. Be sure to wear your Dale Jr. hat for a discount at the door.

A Thought About Gay Marriage

Gays should be allowed to marry. In fact, they should be forced to marry so that they can be just as miserable as everybody else.

Military

Navy, Air Force, DEA, CIA, FBI, ATF – Pick any three letters of the alphabet and you will find them here. You may be wondering just what the military could possibly have to do with making Key West such a great place. Well, wonder no more. Our classroom obtained a recently declassified CIA memo explaining just that.

Strategic Importance of US Military in Maintaining Key West Paradise.

It has been determined that ████████████████████ for the ████████████████ swhich in turn leads to a dramatic and ████████████████ including ████████, and beaches. Global positioning ████████ with the presence of beautiful people and tropical drinks. ████████ therefore making military presence crucial in maintaining paradise.

Makes sense, doesn't it? And let's be honest. In these uncertain times it is nice to know that Key West houses enough fire power to invade a small country and steal all of their rum, should the need arise. More on that subject next semester in Rum Running and Drug Smuggling 101. Cuba, take warning!

Carl the Crazy Conch says:

During the Civil War, Key West was part of the Union. It was the only place in the United States at the time from which you had to travel North to join the South.

10 Celebrities

Speaking from experience, we can tell you that being a celebrity is not all glitz and glamour. It is tough work being famous, earning insane amounts of money and being pursued by groupies. It's difficult to find much more than a moment of "self time" to collect your thoughts and work on your next bestseller. Luckily we can always escape to the Keys.

Key West is a favorite spot among our celebrity friends. We like the tropical climate and late-night party scene, but the best part about it is the people in this town have never adopted that "crazed fan who must create a stampede and shout the celebrity's name at the top of their lungs" mentality. This behavior has paid off, because we tell our celebrity friends it is a chill place, they tell two friends who each tell two friends, and pretty soon the island is crawling with celebrities. In addition to the Sloan – Shultz powerhouse, many other Hollywood A-lister's have decided to call Key West home. Do the names Kelly McGillis, Shel Silverstein, Hulk Hogan and Ernest Hemingway ring a bell? We know things about them that the tabloids never will, thus creating an understanding and respect between the celebrity and the common man not to be found elsewhere this side of the Mississippi. We'll let you ponder that for a moment. Jimmy Buffett's at the door and needs to borrow a cup of sugar.

A Kennedy Kind of Town

In October 1995 Monroe County was briefly renamed Marilyn Monroe county to honor the Fantasy Fest theme: Tinsel Town Dreams…lights, camera, fantasy.

Locals

Local residents, local color, local characters, the local who keeps leering at your teenage daughter... Call us what you want, but be sure to give credit to the people who keep the weird blood pumping through the heart of this crazy paradise wonderland. Locals are different from Conchs in the simple fact that they are born outside of Key West. They also don't drink as much Bud Light. The only requirement for being a local is first, last and security or a friend with a vacant couch accompanied by the lack of desire or funding to reach any destination north of the Seven Mile Bridge. Being a local carries great responsibility. While work is optional, you must attend the occasional sunset, mingle with the tourists to ensure they have the best vacation possible, and come up with at least one story per week about how you drank so much you ended up passing out on the neighbor's front porch with a plastic chicken under your arm and the phone number of someone named Oklahoma. Get to know your locals. They are the ones who will tell you the best places to eat, point you toward the hidden snorkeling spots, and keep an eye on your daughter when she comes back down for spring break.

Get to Know the Locals

Buy them a drink.
Ask directions and buy them a drink.
Offer to sleep with them and buy them a drink.
Buy them a drink.

12 Cats

Cats did not make the original Key West class schedule, but Dr. Jekyll (David's Cat) peed on the manuscript, pooped under our pillows and gave us the silent treatment until we reluctantly agreed to include our feline friends on their very own page. The cat population of Key West has many things going for it, including an endless supply of shady nap spots and plenty of geckos and rats to hone their hunting skills. They also have an unending supply of tourists anxious to pet them, and the ability to mate with their cousins without worrying what their friends and family may think. They owe it all to Ernest Hemingway. His cats were so into sleeping with their cousins that the gene pool became cloudy and they started growing extra toes. Key West cats may be standoffish at times, but they know marketing. That is why we call them Hemingway cats when they are, in fact, incestuous retards.

Ever notice a cat with a little notch taken out of its ear? These are cats that have been humanely trapped and inhumanely separated from their naughty bits. After the operation their ear is notched and they are released back in the wild to romp with their cousins risk free of having pesky kittens. Not bad for an animal that gets blamed for all the missing tongues.

Just a Thought

People are too anxious to use famous people's names to describe something. If a cat wants to be a Hemingway cat, we say having six toes is not enough. They should write a book or two – even a short story, and they should drink and go hunting. If they are really dedicated they should move to Ketcham, Idaho and shoot themselves in the head. That would be a true Hemingway cat!

13 Street Musicians

A famous person once said "music is the soundtrack of the human soul." Okay, it was us – and you can thank God that there is more of a demand for street musicians than cheesy street quotationists. Could you imagine taking a leisurely stroll down Duval Street and suddenly being assaulted by the wit and wisdom of Chris and David? Just the other day we were walking down to Margaritaville having a completely heterosexual quarrel. Things were getting heated and we were about to call off our date with the cheeseburger in paradise when the sweet sounds from an out-of-tune guitar with slightly off-key vocals spoke the words of the late, great Bob Marley. "Don't worry, 'bout a thing, every little thing, is gonna be all right." Suddenly our moods lightened, we kissed and made up (in a very non-gay way) and enjoyed the hell out of our Buffett buffet. A valuable lesson was learned that day, so take notes on our reasoning. It would be hard to place a value on the service provided to us by the dirty little hippie who sang the words that changed our day. Hard indeed, but we figured he would settle for a quarter. Then again, you never know when you might need a quarter for the parking meter, and we like to keep our dimes so we stiffed him. The lesson to be learned? The best things in life are free. If you see a hippie playing Bob Marley on Duval Street, give him a dollar and tell him Chris and David are not gay.

Local Advice

If you're going to smash a guitar into a million pieces
be sure to follow up with a proper apology.

14 Birds

● ●

Birds have been a source of amusement and amazement since we first learned to read from that big yellow one on Sesame Street. His time would have been better spent warning us about the high cost of alcoholism, but he is a bird and birds don't have addictive personalities. Key West has more birds than Sesame Street, but they lack the moral fortitude of Big Bird. Use caution when looking for them in the sky because the birds down here have developed pin point accuracy when it comes to dropping a birdy-bomb on your nose or your freshly washed scooter. We have egrets, spoonbills, loons, herons, peacocks, chickens, an emu and a variety of shoulder birds. All of them poop, and for a couple of dollars you can have your picture taken on Duval Street as a parrot or cockatoo messes your shirt. Our feathered friends do bring us sweet songs, cause to wonder at the amazement of flight and no tropical environment would be complete without them. Plus it is fun to watch them poop on people, so long as it is not you. This lesson was brought to you by the letters K and W and the number 2.

Just be glad we don't have any flying snufalupaguses.

Nikita Khruschev Says:

"If one cannot catch the bird of paradise,
better take a wet hen."

Key West Characters

A step beyond the local color lies the Key West Character. These people are so unique, so true to themselves and so much stranger than the average Key West resident that they have taken on a character all their own that people have come to accept and expect on their visits to the Southernmost Island. The Cookie Lady, Captain Outrageous, Mushroom Mary, The Chicken Lady, Snowball and Spooky Dave are just a few of the names often accompanied by unique outfits and odd dancing. They are everywhere in the Keys, always have been and probably always will be. The names may change but the stories stay the same. This wacky blood is somehow attracted to Key West and helps give the island a sense of vivaciousness and fun. Not only are these people fearless when it comes to creativity, self expression, and karaoke, they also inspire others to be themselves. Their pockets may not be full of money but they are full of life and that's what living in paradise is all about. Watch these characters and learn that paradise is all about you…and the weather.

Carl the Crazy Conch Says:

Back in the days of free love and psychedelics, the hippie kids would hang out at Mallory Square. Straight-laced folk went to watch their antics and a sunset celebration was born.

16 Geckos

• •

Geckos were invading the living rooms of Key West long before the advent of television when ad execs started using them to sell auto insurance. Geckos are the fun little lizards that are everywhere in Key West. They eat bugs, hop around on plants, sell insurance and make a noise from their throat that sounds like "GEKKOOO." This may have something to do with how they got their name.

Our friend Barbara Anderson just called. We told her not to interrupt us while we were writing and she asked us to mention her in the book. Barbara Anderson knows nothing about geckos but she will sell you a great piece of commercial property. The little lizards take some getting used to if you come from the North. They will treat your house as their own, so the key is not to think of them as slithery little snake-like creatures, but more like pet dinosaurs with the ability to climb walls and grow new tails. The dinosaur thing provides hours of entertainment – especially if you are really high. Did you know geckos are territorial? One could take up residence in your mailbox for several months, or you may notice a particular fellow scurrying across your doorstep every time you leave the house. People in Key West have been known to name their geckos, and for some reason "Bob" is the name of choice. There is a famous gecko named Bob who lives on Olivia Street near the cemetery. Legend has it that he fell from a tree and hit his throat, so now every time he talks it sounds like he is saying "F*%K YOOU!" Let's see the car insurance people top that one!

Names besides Bob that people have given their adopted gecko

1. Stanley   2. Jecho the Gecko
3. Liz   4. Fire Truck

Chris and David
The famous authors of this book

Did you know Key West was once inhabited by Indians? They probably don't like being called Indians now but it is impossible to keep up with political correctness in the publishing industry and we are not going to update this book every three months. Our apologies to all of the red men with funny animal names, but back to Chris and David. There was an ancient Indian prophecy found scrawled on the walls of a cave near Fort Taylor that told of the coming of two great writers to the island. The prophecy went so far as to identify the writers by name. While there are thousands of people living in Key West who have helped to make this such a great place, this is our book – not theirs, so allow us to toot our own horns for a moment. Without us the island would not have such great books as Quit Your Job and Move to Key West, Ghosts of Key West and all of the great titles that Phantom Press will be publishing in the coming years. Not only do we capture the heart, soul and humor of this crazy island, we put it in a compact, affordable package that you can take home to your friends. As for the Indian prophecy, their names were Ernest and Tennessee. Lucky for us, both of them are dead now and the road has been paved for the Key West Kings of Bathroom Books. Think how shallow and meaningless your daily visit to the Key West bathroom would be without us. I guess you could say without Chris and David you would be shit out of luck. Now let's take a pee break before we move on to the next reason.

Places you're most likely to run into the fabulous Chris and David:
Grand Vin, the cemetery, behind the magazine store, yo mama's house.

photo: RobONeal.com

25

What's the Function?

photo: RobONeal.com

18 2 x 4 Mile Island

Three Mile Island may have been enough for Pennsylvania, but when it comes to measuring your peninsula, size really does matter. Luckily for us, smaller is better – at least that's what we lead our girlfriends to believe. Maybe that's why they keep dumping us for chicks. We know this because the island is small. This means everything is close by, a taxi never costs more than ten bucks, the beach is always in walking distance and the next bar is usually less than a block away. People can't back out of an appointment because they are stuck in traffic on the other side of town. If you lose someone's phone number you will definitely bump into them again, and secrets of size become common knowledge. They say no man is an island, but if we were, we would be Key West; small, warm and slightly detached.

Reasons Women Should Date David and Chris Instead of Other Women

1. We are famous authors and you can write a tell-all book about us when we hit it really big.
2. We are men and we have needs.
3. Street lights often go out when Chris walks by.
4. Wow the folks with your intimate knowledge of David's Ween tattoo.

19 Flora and Fauna

Key West would not be the same without Flora and Fauna. They are twin sisters from Nebraska with smiles that could stop a war and baby blue eyes that could melt a snowman in December. The most incredible thing happened on the night of January 22, 1999. The twins had just come back to town wearing nothing but little pink... Wow, do we feel stupid. Our editor just informed us that flora and fauna are scientific terms for plants and stuff. This won't be nearly as interesting as the twins story, but we are told we must stick with the subject or they will cut out our liquor allowance. One of the great joys of living in Key West is walking down a side street after years of living in town and discovering a plant you have never seen before. Key West is bursting with different varieties of plants and flowers from all around the world, now available in different colors, smells, shapes and sizes. Mangoes, bananas, coconuts, avocados, banyans, poincianas and more palms than you can shake a frond at. They provide limitless enjoyment and it doesn't cost you a thing, which reminds us, we need to get back to the twins. Enjoy the plant life, nature boy.

Carl the Crazy Conch Says:

Key West's Tropical Forest and Botanical Garden is the only frost-free one of its kind in the continental United States. It is home to many endangered and threatened species and a major stopping point for traveling neo-tropical birds.

Parks

Anybody who played Monopoly as a child learned at an early age that the banker always wins and Boardwalk was useless if you didn't have Park Place. The same can be said for this giant Monopoly board we call Key West, and lucky for us we have parks galore – not an easy accomplishment in a place where an acre of land is worth a million dollars. There are big parks for baseball, soccer and football, smaller parks for boccie and hibachi, and "pocket parks" hidden all over the island. Can't decide between the park and the beach? Head to Fort Zachary Taylor state park and you can enjoy the best of both worlds complete with a Civil War-era fort to explore. What can you do in these parks? Almost anything. Some people play with their pets, some people stretch or meditate, and others just lay back and chill or read a good book like this one. The only thing limiting you is your imagination. Throughout history, parks have been a favorite place to get high, but you should be warned that in the Key West game of Monopoly there are no "get out of jail free" cards. No free parking either.

Carl the Crazy Conch Says:

Fort Zachary Taylor was active during the
Civil War, the Spanish-American War, World War I and
World War II. The Fort's ghosts have been seen
re-creating battles to this day.

21 Salt Ponds

• •

To the untrained eye, the Salt Ponds may appear to be just another marshy area dwarfed by the beauty of the Atlantic Ocean and rampant condo development, but a little history behind the reason for the season will spice things up a bit and you will be peppered with more facts than a salty sea dog. Key West has been blessed with the absence of anything resembling cold weather, but in the days before refrigeration this presented some problems if you didn't have a taste for rotten meat. Faced with the problem of eating an entire cow in one sitting or dining on spoiled meat and spending a week in the outhouse, the resourceful people of Key West adopted the tradition of curing their meats with salt. This was done by containing the sea water at high tide in a retention pond, allowing the water to evaporate and leaving behind... salt. So successful was the process that people started seeking other uses for their beloved salt. Maybe it would take the bite out of the tequila, let's try it on these exploded corn kernels. What do you say we throw it over our shoulders for good luck? We talked before about paradise soup. If your soup is tasting a little bland, just add salt. Tequila and limes are optional.

Take It With a Grain of Salt

On October 19, 1876 a hurricane washed away over 15,000 bushels of ungathered salt ending all future attempts of salt making by solar evaporation in Key West.

 # Sunrise

When Hemingway wrote "The Sun Also Rises" he was probably letting the people of Key West know that sunset was not the only game in town. We wouldn't know because we never read Hemingway. While the Key West sunset sold out and went commercial long ago, we can take great satisfaction in the fact that the sunrise has stuck to its traditional roots and not sold its soul (sol) to make a quick buck. To honor this great achievement, we propose staying up all night drinking with friends and heading to the beach at the crack of dawn to applaud sunrise's achievement. It is a magical experience. Sunrise has no celebration, no street performers, not too many tourists and no T-shirt shops. It has a soothing effect on the soul and everything feels fresh and new as the sun paints the island to life. Feeling creative? Bring along a bottle of Cuervo and have your very own Tequila Sunrise. Old Ernest would be proud.

Grandma Knows Best

"With each sunrise a new day begins, so who cares about the crap that happened yesterday or what crap will happen tomorrow."
~ Chris's Grandma

Sunset

Funny how we slam the sunset in the section about sunrises and return less than a page later to sing its praises. We have also been known to criticize people's drinking habits with a beer in hand. It's called a double standard and you should get used to it if you want to be our friend. Key West is famous for its sunsets. Every night the magical hour hits the islands and time slows down as the sun melts into the ocean. We are so enamored with sunsets that an entire celebration has been built around them and can be enjoyed from the carnival atmosphere of Mallory Square and the Hilton, the bird's-eye view from the La Concha, the bar's eye view from the Schooner Wharf, or the unhampered oceanfront view from a sunset sail aboard a schooner. There is a feeling of paradise in the air as the fiery ball begins her descent into the ocean bringing a close to the day and ushering in the adventures of night that await us. The sunset is so spectacular the people can't help but applaud it. Be sure to do the same. We will be the drunk guys in the back making fun of the people who come to watch the sunset and criticizing your drinking habits.

Hip To Be Square

Mallory Square was once the site of
a boarding house run by Ellen Mallory.

Climate

When the sun is shining and the weather is sweet 95 percent of the time, life seems pretty damn good. Welcome to the weather of Key West. Oddly enough, this is one of the most popular reasons people come here and has resulted in those humorous postcards with the Jimmy Buffett line "The weather is here, wish you were beautiful." The average year-round temperature is about 79 degrees, which happens to be the ideal temperature for fishing, volleyball, long walks on the beach and Christmas morning in your shorts. Make sure to put the lights on the palm tree and keep plenty of suntan lotion for the elves in bikinis. The weather is also a great conversation starter in Key West and a simple comment about the beautiful clouds in the sky can easily lead to an afternoon of action and adventure with a new friend. One word to the wise: Be careful when referring to the temperature, as there are plenty of people on the island who will be more than happy to take your temperature where the sun don't shine. This is an example of another time you don't want to be the butt of a joke.

Let It Rain

Storms don't bother us. Our drinks have umbrellas!

25 Beaches

If you have spent much time checking out the beaches in Key West you are probably questioning the validity of including this item on the list of 101. Even suicidal whales know that attempting a Key West beaching will result in more water than sand and a greater probability of a staph infection than death. We don't have miles of pristine sand like you see in the brochures and on book covers, but what do you expect? The photo on "Quit Your Job and Move to Key West" was taken in Cuba, but we like to look at the glass as half full. There is a wonderful beach at Fort Zachary Taylor State Park where all of the locals go. It is a short bike ride away from Old Town and boasts one of the coolest low sand beaches you will ever visit. Shaded by pine trees and perfect for hanging in a hammock, a day at Fort Zachary Taylor will bring you down to a good speed. Swim out to the rocks for a snorkel with the sea creatures or just chill on the jetty and catch rays with the gulls. Riding the current from one end to the other rivals any lazy river experience and the movement keeps the water fresh and clean. For your viewing pleasure there are boats sailing in the distance, jet skis cruising by, and a pretty good selection of bathing beauties. Our beaches may not be the French Riviera, but they beat the hell out of that Bette Midler movie our moms keep making us watch.

Beach Bums

You never know how many friends you have
until you rent a house on the beach.

26 Duval Street

Known as the longest street in the world because it stretches from the Gulf of Mexico to the Atlantic Ocean, Duval Street is the main artery in the heart of Key West. Bars, restaurants, art galleries, T-shirt shops, gift boutiques, sex stores and water sports depots are just a few of the life-bloods that sustain this lane and if you can't find it here or find out about it here, it probably doesn't exist. The street takes its name from Florida Governor William P. Duval who, like the street, is described as short, with a ruddy countenance and a genial manner accompanied by a wit and humor that made him the life of every party. He was also a member of the bar. Duval was born in Virginia. At age 16 he was sitting in the living room with his family and some neighbors when his father came in and lectured him sharply for a neglect of duty, concluding by saying, "Get up from that chair, you good for nothing and bring in a log for the fire!" On his way to the log pile, William decided since he was a good for nothing, he would set out and make something of himself. Without even saying goodbye he jumped on his horse and headed south. He studied the bar, was sent to congress and appointed governor, then nearly 20 years later he returned to his childhood home. As he approached the house, the now-famous governor grabbed a log from the yard, entered the room where his family and some neighbors were gathered, and after placing the log in the fire to his satisfaction said, "Here is the log you asked me to fetch father." "Well" answered the father, "You were long enough getting it!"

photo: RobONeal.com

Carl the Crazy Conch Says:

A traditional tour of Duval Street known as "The Duval Crawl"
is a good way for you to pay tribute to the governor. The idea
is to start at one end of the street and work your way to the
other, stopping in every bar along the way to get a drink. It
doesn't take long for most people to wind up on their hands and
knees with their liver trailing by three blocks. If you want to make
things interesting, try carrying a log. Make it from one end to the
other, and like Governor Duval, you have passed the bar exam.

37

27 Hidden Lanes

• •

How long should it take before you know all the streets of Key West like the palm of your hand? We know our palms pretty well, so it never ceases to amaze us, after years of island living, when these little gems pop up. We are talking about the lanes again, so get your mind out of the gutter. The island has a way of hiding these beauties from you until the time is right. Just when you thought you had seen it all and were ready to move on to bigger and better places, out pops a flower-lined lane with hidden cottages you have passed a million times but never seemed to notice. Cruising down it creates a trippy twilight-zone-like feeling and it is hard to restrain yourself from jumping in the air and exclaiming, "I'm Ponce De *$%* Leon !" These simple finds make your problems disappear. The world is suddenly a bigger place as your worries and troubles slip away into a little Norman Rockwell Lane that was discovered by you.

Carl the Crazy Conch Says:

If want to take a guided tour of the hidden lanes, check out Lloyd's Key West Nature Bike Tour. Call 305-294-1882 and tell Lloyd Carl the Crazy Conch sent ya!

28 Bahama Village

One of the last few pieces of Old Key West, Bahama Village is located a couple blocks off Duval Street and boasts one of the quaintest communities on the island. Bahamian tradition is the backbone of this neighborhood and generation after generation of family knows their neighbor, their neighbor's mama and their mama's mama too. In the past several years the houses have started selling to outsiders and gentrification is a serious concern, but the neighborhood still boasts the soul of its past. One of the mainstays in Bahama Village is Blue Heaven Restaurant. This eclectic four-star restaurant is world famous for its food, atmosphere and of course, the chickens. The good news is, you don't have to die to get there. Another culinary delight centers around Goombay Festival, a two-day event celebrating Bahamian food, art and, of course, beer. This is the first festival after a long hot summer and it brings out the locals and Conchs in droves. Imagine a high school reunion on acid, except your girlfriend's dress doesn't keep melting into the floor. Wear loose pants to this one because you will definitely be packing on the pounds. Spend enough time in the village and people will start to recognize you. Mr. Chapman has got his eye on everything, making sure everyone is on the up and up. What else would you expect from a man with a street named after him?

Carl the Crazy Conch Says:

Key West's Bahama Village neighborhood sits on the island's original settlement. Our sister city is Green Turtle Cay, Bahamas.

29 Hurricanes

• •

What could a hurricane possibly have to do with paradise, you ask? Good question, considering that on the surface they appear to be good for little more than death and destruction and tracking their path is a far cry from a science. So destructive is their capacity that we have designated a hurricane season, but just like women's basketball, we don't pay much attention to what's happening. Back in 1922 a nun by the name of Sister Gabriel built a grotto located at Saint Mary's Star Of The Sea Chapel. Upon dedicating it to the people of Key West she declared that so long as the grotto stands Key West will never suffer the full brunt of a major hurricane. Her prayers worked, making hurricanes avoid Key West like the plague and keeping us wishing we hadn't skipped Sunday school on the day they were talking about protective spells. Now we are free to enjoy the benefits of mandatory evacuation, such as no work, no tourists, hurricane parties, and an excess of food that will go bad if the restaurants don't give it away. Some reason remains of course, and we realize that there is a possibility we could be swept off the face of the globe, so all good Key West residents stock up on booze and cuddle up with the first available cutie. "If you can't be with the one you love, love the one you're with." It's okay, baby, there's a hurricane coming.

Carl the Crazy Conch Says:

The official Atlantic hurricane season runs from
June 1 through November 30.

30 Tropical Breezes

It is a shame that the term "breeze" has been hijacked by the people who make laundry detergents and feminine hygiene products, but it was bound to happen when a word appeared in the English language describing such a delightful, yet unobtainable thing. Wind usually gets a bad rap, especially when it involves Chris and vegetarian cuisine. Nobody likes gusts and we complain if it's windy, but send in a breeze and the problems of the world seem to gently lift away. Key West has taken full advantage of our tropical breezes and we go out of our way to make sure they are enjoyed. Open air bars, wraparound porches, hammocks, convertibles and clothing-optional pools are just a few of our breeze-inspired inventions. Whenever we get back to Key West and step off the plane a tropical breeze hits our face and we know we are home. If the tropical breeze isn't enough, you can add Bahama Breeze, Sea Breeze, Bay Breeze and a number of other cocktails to the list of things that keep us feeling April fresh.

Other Words Ruined by the Feminine Hygiene Industry

Play, Fresh, Comfort, Powder, Cotton, Pad, String

31 Infrastructure

●●●●●●●●●●●●●●●●●●●●●●●●●●●●●●●●●●●●●

We have often wondered what infrastructure means. Is there a head of infrastructure? How do you get the job? How did the roads get connected and who invented the road? Maybe we smoke too much pot and analyze things to death, but at least it pays the bills. We asked a guy on the street named Brad what he thought about the infrastructure. He was kind enough to explain. "Infrastructure is defined as the basic facilities and services for the functioning of a community, such as transportation, communications, water, power and public institutions." Pretty boring stuff for your average Brad, but these are the very things that separate us from all of the third world countries. Every day there is a team of government officials working hard to make sure we are not walking down sewage-filled streets. Not only does it keep the health department off our back, it also ensures Key West's place at the top of the list for second world countries. Our infrastructure may be twisted and loose, but so are our joints and our girlfriends. You don't hear us complaining about them.

Carl the Crazy Conch Says:

Infrastructure shyrmfrastructor!
Who really cares? I like to eat green eggs and ham
with blue cheese. How do you like them apples?

32 Airport

Airports are usually associated with insane traffic, distant parking, lines for the lines and a pretty good chance of getting more action from the security guards than you do from your spouse. Welcome to the Key West airport, where the lines are short, the drinks are tall and we still giggle every time they say cockpit. You know you are in paradise the moment you step off the plane. We don't have those moving tunnels that connect the plane to the terminal, so the second you step out of the craft you get an instant taste of sunshine and island music. You half expect to be met by a man with a midget dressed in white suits and black ties. We don't have the open-air station wagons, but a taxi is always nearby and it never takes more than 15 minutes to get you to your destination. On your return trip to fly out, traffic jams are replaced with ocean views and the average wait for security is only a minute or two. The guards may give you some action, but this is usually only done on request and tipping is customary if they do a good job. Flight delayed? It happens here just like anywhere else, but the bar is in easy reach from both gates one and two. Forget to buy gifts for your friends? The gift shop sells books by famous authors like us. Give the gift that keeps giving. Aim for the window seat on your flight out so you can check out the pristine waters, point out all of the bars you drank in and raise a glass to paradise. If you are good, the captain might even let you in the cockpit. Heh, heh.

Carl the Crazy Conch Says:

If you lose your identification, the DMV is
right next door to the airport.

Homes

● ●

Not everyone has the money to buy a house in Key West, but a home is something we can all afford. Living on a small island, people crave a space that is unique to them, so it should come as no surprise that our residents' condos, apartments, boat cabins and houses are as unique and diverse as the people who live in them. While tourists pay admission to catch a glimpse behind the doors of former residents' homes, locals get to experience the magic on a daily basis without paying a dime. Homes in Key West are like drag queens in that looks can be deceiving, and it is not uncommon to step through the doors of a rundown shack with broken shutters and chipped paint to find a luxurious interior with hardwood floors, marble counter tops and a jacuzzi tub in the middle of the kitchen. Building codes are strict and property taxes are high. This combination has led to a greater focus on the interior while the exterior is left to suffer. The island attitude is ever present in our homes, so expect to be assaulted with an array of tropical colors, funky furniture and decor, plus homemade art. When it comes to home decorating in paradise, everyone is an artist and the place they lay their head at night may start as a blank canvas, but evolves into a masterpiece. It would probably be safe to say that home is where the art is.

Home On the Range

The average price of a for a home will not be printed in this book because it changes daily!

34 Architecture

Real estate ads across the United States boast Key West-style homes, but the architecture of the island is, in fact, a hodgepodge of different styles ranging from Victorian to Caribbean. There is much that can be learned about the history of different houses simply by observing some of the unique architectural features. Some of the earliest homes were actually brought to Key West on boats from the Bahamas and reassembled. Others were constructed by shipbuilders and utilized the same techniques as vessels at sea. The ornate gingerbread carvings adorning many of the homes were once indications of the homeowner's profession and nearly every style took the tropical climate into consideration with plenty of windows and wraparound porches. Tin roofs served a dual purpose as they helped collect clean rain water and did not take to neighboring flames as quickly as their wooden predecessors. Widow's walks provided a view of harbor traffic and sea conditions, and basements were almost non-existent because of elevation problems, requiring the residents to convert other rooms into a bar with a pool table. There are over 3,000 structures in Key West's historic district and every single one contributes to the island's charm.

Carl the Crazy Conch Says:

Key West houses were built to withstand hurricanes, heat and humidity. They often used hand-hewn wood put together with pegs because plaster cracks and decays in high humidity and nails were sometimes scarce.

 # Cuba!

The sign on the Southernmost Point marker reads "90 miles to Cuba," and though this makes it closer than Miami, travel restrictions have turned our relationship with her into a secret affair. The Cuban influence on our island cannot be denied. In addition to the Cuban people, Cuban food and Cuban coffee there is an entire culture and deep-rooted history that stems from our neighboring country. Hundreds of structures in Old Town served as cigar factories or homes for the workers who rolled the Cuban tobacco. The Cuban Club and San Carlos institute on Duval were both hubs of Cuban culture, and La Te Da is an abbreviation for La Terrasa de Marti, named in tribute for a speech Jose Marti gave from the balcony. Even Fidel Castro has been a guest on our tiny island. Activity thrived in our harbors during the Mariel Boat Lift, and speculation continues about the role Key West will play when U.S. restrictions are dropped, opening Cuba for free trade. Some people think our island will be forgotten, but there is a better chance another sign will be added at the Southernmost Point reading "ferry departs every hour."

Bar None

Sloppy Joe's Bar was named by Hemingway
after a bar in Havana where the ice troughs drained
directly onto the floor. The Cuban bar was owned by Jose Garcia.

36 Stock Island

• •

Need a break from Key West? Take a short drive to the next island up for a bit of old-school adventure and fun. Known as the Stock Rock this island was originally used as a holding ground for livestock, thus the names Stock Island and Cow Key Channel, which separates it from Key West. The livestock of yesteryear has been replaced with party animals, and though some people still have a cow when they have to drive all the way out there, this hidden gem is home to shrimp boats, tattoo parlors, hidden bars and some of the best Cuban sandwiches you will ever find, that is if you can find them. The trip is worth it, and that's no bull. As real estate prices continue to skyrocket in Key West, developers are horning in and have turned their attention to the greener pastures of Stock Island, where you can still find the occasional trailer in the half million dollar range. When you have finished choking on your Cuban sandwich, start talking to a mortgage lender; the same trailer may be worth a million by the time this class is dismissed and even Bill Gates could be priced out of the market in a few years. Until that day, we'll enjoy that edge-of-the world feeling you get on the back docks surrounded by people who probably have a prison record and won't tell you their last names. They don't have a beef with you, but this is no place for cow-ards. These puns are getting cheesy, so I guess we have milked them enough. Didn't mean to get your goat. We were just kidding. That was baaad.

Local Advice

Be sure to have a light on your bike at night. The cops like to pull you over and search you for goodies!

History

Yawn. High school history class reminds us of the year we were addicted to Rohyponal and worked as male escorts: No chance to sleep, weekly tests, and bunch of dates we didn't care about and can't seem to remember. You probably had a similar experience, but Key West knows how to put the story in his-story, so wake up from your nap, wipe the drool from your chin and kick back for a history lesson with more tales than the Playboy mansion. Ponce de Leon and the fountain of youth, the Bermuda Triangle, pirates, voodoo, wreckers, shrimpers, tourists, rumrunners, politicians, priests... Key West history has it all and most of it rolls off your tongue like a story over a campfire with a couple of beers. Every corner in Key West is filled with some magically strange tale of human surprise or mystery and you can feel the soul of the island every time you leave your house. It's like the spirits of history are still there waiting for their stories to be told. It does not take much to get the history of Key West. Just like getting any other kind of solid information, we highly recommend grabbing a seat at the local bar. Our history lives in the hearts of the locals and a world of adventure can unfold for the price of a few drinks. You might even run into a few dates worth remembering.

Local Advice

Don't ask your waiter if he lives in Key West.
Stupid questions lead to smart-ass answers.

38 Big Cities

How deep is your love for Key West? You may have heard the term "island fever" used to describe the condition where one of the voices in your head tries to convince you that Key West is not all that. This is not the kind of fever John Travolta gets on a Saturday night where you feel the need to pimp out in a white suit and your favorite pair of disco shoes. It's the kind that makes you shiver and sweat and is often accompanied by a nasty case of diarrhea. There is only one cure for this kind of fever and it involves a giant dose of big-city mayhem. Every time we end up in Miami, Japan, London or see the Manhattan Skyline while jetting around on a book-signing tour, it reminds us why we call Key West home. The hustle and bustle of these cities drives us mad and we can't help but wonder how people are stayin' alive dealing with traffic jams, corporate takeovers, screw you attitudes, jive talkin' and bad coffee. People actually judge you by what you wear and how much money you make? Life is too short to argue, you should be dancin'. We miss our girlfriends too, but Key West is more than a woman. Thank God we have Calgon to take us away and a return ticket to paradise waiting in the breast pocket of our white disco suit.

Local Advice

Try not to sleep with locals if you live here. You have to see them all the time and if you're bad in bed everyone will know. Stick with tourists. They leave in the morning.

Secret Spots

Why do you always have to make things sexual? If you want to know about that secret spot, pick up a book on the Kama Sutra or sign up for sex ed. We are here to talk about the hidden parts of Key West that the tourists don't know about and the locals won't share. Living on a small island has its benefits, but everyone needs some time alone to relax with mother nature in a way that a crowded beach can't satisfy. This is where the hidden gardens, secluded courtyards, up-the-Keys coves and stray trails come into play. Spots to go where you don't have to give directions, say hi to people whose names you can't remember or buy a drink to enjoy the atmosphere. Everyone needs a place to slow down, escape reality and soothe their troubled soul – even in Key West. "Where are these spots?" you ask. Find your own damn spot. They wouldn't be much of a secret if we blabbed about them to you and the last thing we need is someone interrupting us for an autograph while we talk to the geckos about our inner child. So get off your lazy butt and take a walk or a bike ride to discover one on your own. These spots are there, but discovering them is half the fun as they take on a personal meaning that will enrich your time in Key West. The longer you have them, the more special they become. Don't tell your friends, don't tell a soul. It is no secret that the geckos like to talk so if you and your friend have the same secret spot, the geckos will blab to him, he'll get drunk and blab to the bartender, the bartender will blab to your significant other and before you know it the entire town will know about your inner child's obsession with finding the g-spot. So much for secrets.

Local Advice

Don't listen to the voice in your head that tells you to help out the police with their investigation.

40 Conch Republic

The Conch Republic is such a vast subject, entire books have been written about it. Shakespeare wrote a lot of books too, but we always got by just fine with Cliff's notes, so today we are proud to present the Conch Republic in a nutshell. Around 1982 drug trafficking in the Keys was running rampant. The government set up a roadblock near Miami and searched every car that left the Keys. Four-hour traffic jams did not sit well with the tourists so they stopped coming down. This meant no money, so the only happy people were the drug users in Key West, but that is to be expected when supply exceeds demand in such overwhelming proportions. The local politicians who didn't do drugs were not amused so they seceded from the Union, named Key West the Conch Republic, declared war on the United States and began an assault on the mainland with conch fritters and stale Cuban bread. The war was short-lived as the new republic immediately surrendered and requested millions of dollars in aid. We didn't get the money but the roadblock came down and we were free to traffic drugs without the hassle of those pesky DEA agents. The tourists started coming back, and today we have our own passport, flag and souvenir cups. We even have a Hard Rock Cafe! Every year there is a Conch Republic Independence celebration, which is not to be missed. Just don't go quoting any Shakespeare or we'll whack you in the head with a conch fritter.

Local Advice

Don't stick your privates in the coconuts.
It's rude and you most likely will get a rash.

Location

Do you know the three 'L's of real estate? Location, location, location. This really upsets us because even a retard knows that there is only one 'L' in the word and it comes right after the 'R' the 'E' and the 'A'. If the person who came up with this saying could stop stuttering for a minute and learn to count, they would have known that there are three 'E's. Everyone is fascinated with location. Where are you from? Which state? Which city? What section? Which street? We like to start broad and narrow things down until we run out of things to talk about and can move on to new people with different locations to pinpoint. Mild complaining aside, Key West has one of the greatest locations in the world: the Southernmost Point of the Continental United States. Longitude and latitude have been kind to our island as you might have noticed in our weather, our water and our ability to dodge hurricanes. We are just far enough from the mainland to feel like a third world country, but close enough still to reap the rewards of federal grants, paved roads and indoor plumbing. Another 90 miles south and we would all be speaking Spanish. Just think how the 'L's would roll off our tongues then.

Local Advice

Don't wear black socks with sandals,
unless you're German.

42 Mile Markers

We would like to put an end to all the confusion caused by these strange green signs with numbers on them dotting the highway. They are not exit signs. They are not depth markers like you see on the side of your pool, and they are not a guideline for how many beers should be left in your cooler as you head towards Key West. The mile markers are "markers" to designate the "mile." Technical stuff, we know, but you will get the hang of it. U.S.1 starts in Fort Kent, Maine and continues all the way down to MM0 in Key West. You can drive it if you want, but Maine is cold and the route is full of traffic lights, so we suggest a flight into Miami and a rental car to paradise, as all of the good numbers are down here anyway. 100, 86, 69, 3 – we have them all and 0 too. You can buy MM0 souvenirs to mark your historic journey, or if you are feeling dangerous, steal the real sign like everybody else. Put it by your pool at the shallow end.

Less than Zero

The upper half of Whitehead Street is often in better repair than the bottom half because the federal government stops paving at Mile Marker 0 but the road continues another six blocks.

 **Jobs**

• •

Juggling, painting, telling stories, driving a train; we actually get paid to do this stuff. While the rest of the world draws a prominent line between work and play, the people of Key West have managed to blend the two into a tasty tropical drink that occupies our time and allows us to earn a few bucks doing what we love. On one end of the scale you will find Bird Man, Iguana Guy, Sword Swallower and the rest of the gang down at Sunset Celebration. They are masters of their craft and leave a lasting impression on everyone they encounter. On the other end of the scale you will find accountants, secretaries, realtors and office workers. Not everyone is a Key West character, and these people provide the valuable services that keep our island ticking. In between are the writers, artists, small business owners, bartenders and tourist trade workers. Whether we work from nine 'til five or from 6:30 p.m. 'til sunset, every job in the Keys has a relaxed dress code, a slower pace and an island attitude. We don't do TPS reports.

Local Advice

For the most comprehensive look a the job market and employment statistics we highly recommend picking up Chris and David's first book "Quit You Job and Move to Key West."

44 Cruise ships

• •

There are three schools of thought when it comes to cruise ships visiting Key West. The first group loves them and consists of businesses who reap the rewards of 2,000 people being herded onto the island with only six hours to spend their $32. The second group hates them because they don't get any of the $32 and the third group is not aware that we even have a cruise ship pier in Key West. As the cruising industry continues to boom, more ships are making Key West a port of call. Disney, Royal Caribbean and Carnival all make stops here, docking either at Mallory Square, the Hilton Pier or the Outer Mole, which was a dock for Navy ships recently purchased by the City. With the cruise ships come environmental concerns, most of them surrounding water quality or quality of life. All of those kamikazes they drink have to go somewhere, and a few thousand extra people peeing in the toilets at Sloppy Joe's can put a strain on the system. The employees don't care for it much either, especially after asparagus night on the ship. Most boats don't stay overnight because we don't like them blocking the sunset. We wish them bon voyage as they pull away, watch the sun go down and figure out which bar to spend their 32 bucks in.

A Boat Load

More than 660,000 cruise ship passengers
visit Key West every year.

Hot Fun In the Summer Time!

photo: RobONeal.com

 # Drinks

The drink is believed to be so satisfying because it incorporates all six of your senses. The sight of the liquid as it spills into your glass, the smell of the rum as you raise the glass to your nose, the taste of the oak as it rolls across your tongue and the sound of the glasses as you clink a toast to paradise. What about the sixth sense, you ask. That is your psychic sense predicting a hangover in your future if you keep drinking at this pace. (Coming Soon! The Key West Hangover Survival Guide) Pacing yourself can be tough in Key West because we have such a great variety of drinks. Who can resist a margarita at Margaritaville? How do you say no to a Key West Lager at the very bar where Hemingway drank? Root beer barrel? Sounds good, I think I will try one. Just one more, honey, the bartender has a specialty drink. If anyone thinks you are drinking too much and asks what you think you are doing, take a look at your glass, lift it to your nose, take a sip and make a toast. Then tell them you have finally come to your senses. Wow them with your psychic ability while you are at it, and have a drink for us. We predict we will be at the bar soon.

Cheers

"Drink what you want, drink what you're able,
if you're drinking with us, you'll be under the table"
~ David and Chris

46 Stars

They say the stars at night are big and bright (rednecks clap here) deep in the heart of Texas. We're not going to argue about stars with the Texans – they are probably packing a weapon- but we would like to add Key West to the list. Take a stroll through the streets of Old Town on a clear night, gaze up at the sky and watch these babies come alive. They are not necessarily brighter or more visible than out on a country road or a boat in the middle of the ocean, but they do take on a different meaning. It is as though you are walking with them and they are a part of you. It could have something to do with the fact that we are usually loaded by the time the sun goes down, but we checked this out with some sober people and they assured us we were not crazy, just before kicking us off of their porch and threatening to call the cops. A bike ride down the beach side of the island offers a great view of the sky and the Atlantic Ocean, and the view from a sailboat provides the perfect backdrop to remind us just how small we really are... in case the Texans have not done that already.

Starstruck

Hemingway's second son, Patrick, taught himself the constellations from a book on the roof of the family's Whitehead Street home.

Sports

• •

You may not expect much in the way of athletics from an island where drinking and sunbathing are the main sports, but Key West does have some normal activities. Shoot your sister, toss the keg, ride the dolphin and box the clown are just a few of the more popular ones, but you will also find the typical ball sports. On any given weeknight there is the Southernmost Bocce League. All you need are three or four friends and a case of beer (each) to have a ball hanging out on a dirt path with a bunch of goofballs rolling balls at each other's balls. It's not as bad as it sounds. They even host a ball at the end of season. If tossing balls in the dirt is not your thing, you can toss balls at a bat in the softball league or kick a ball with one of the soccer teams. Still not floating your boat? Hit some balls on the tennis courts, fight over the ball in a big pile of men with our rugby league or join one of the martial arts schools and learn how to kick someone in the balls more effectively. No matter what sport you choose, always remember to bring your own equipment. There is nothing worse than being forced to play with someone else's balls.

Other Things We Like To Do With Our Balls

1 Throw them in a hoop.
2. Roll them at pins.
3. Take them to the beach.
4. Throw them to our dog.
5. Keep them clean for the next time we use them.

48 Outer islands

Snipes, Marvin, Marquesa. These are not the stars of the latest Hollywood blockbuster, but you will need to know them to enjoy the paradise matinee. These are some of the outer islands that surround Key West, and most of them are only accessible by private boat. If you don't have a boat you will need a friend who has one, the cash to rent one, or a damn good backstroke. If you do have a boat, the outer islands will provide countless afternoons of exploration with nature, solitude from the hustle of the big island, and a good excuse to drink beer naked. There are more islands than we would know to name, but any fishing guide worth his weight in salt can steer you to the ones where you are welcome. Some are privately owned and others environmentally protected, so check for barking dogs or monkeys flinging poo before hanging your hammock. When the coast is clear, sit back and take in the pristine waters, tropical views, bountiful fishing, and snorkeling that is second to none. The cinematography is out of this world.

Message in a Bottle

The music in the theme song for Gillian's Island
was actually written for "I Dream Of Jeannie."

Fitness

Every time we talk about fitness the song "Let's Get Physical" pops into our heads. Olivia Newton John is always close behind and before you know it our Grease 25th Anniversary limited edition DVD is cranking on the television and we are running around the living room pantomiming "The One That I Want" and freaking out the dog. The great thing about Key West is there are countless ways to get physical. Ride your bike, walk everywhere, jog around the island, do some yoga, swim, join the gym, take a dance class or come to one of our Grease parties. If your self motivation is running low, get a job that will make you get fit. Drive a pedicab, guide snorkel trips, mate on a sail boat (not that kind of mating, you sick puppy), or lead a walking tour. Bartenders never seem to have a spare tire, but the special diet powder ingested through their noses keeps them looking in tip top shape. Despite rumors, too much grease is not bad for you. Stay fit and your body will be hopelessly devoted to you.

Carl the Crazy Conch Says:

The advantage to working out every single day
is that you die healthier.

Art

• •

Key West is known as the island of the arts and that's no joke. You can hardly leave your house without stumbling into an art form as there are painters, street musicians and sculptors on near-ly every corner. Art has been a driving force in Key West since the first Bahamian settler painted his porch blue, and every year the artistic community continues to grow stronger. Gallery walks and tours are the norm with new shows opening nearly every week fea-turing everything from painting and sculpting to photography and the art of dance. There is art in our yards, art on our cars, body art, sand sculpture art, a guy named Art and even a K-mart. Key West may be small in size, but when it comes to creative capacity per capita we are, without question, leaders in the field. Want some famous names to back the claim? Van Gogh, Monet, Da Vinci and Picasso never painted here, but compare their works to the likes of Grob, Nowak, McNally and Wyland and we are pretty sure you would prefer to have the art of Key West hanging in your living room. If you are not delighted, you are not paying attention.

**Words Created By
Adding a Letter to Art**

Bart, Cart, Dart, Mart, Part, Tart, Wart, Zart...etc., Hee hee.

Music

Did you hear they combined country music with rap? They call it crap! We don't have time for that nonsense in the islands because we are a little busy trying to come up with a new drinking song that fits in with the three chords we know on guitar. The sounds of our island are a definite reflection of our lifestyle which means there is a predominance of one-chord wonders singing about drinking, fishing, sunshine, tourists and honkytonks. But we would be selling ourselves short if we didn't expose our other talents. We're not talking about our tap skills or our unique ability to drink an entire pint of Guinness while standing on our heads, but of the incredible musical talent that lies hidden in the Key West underground. There are jazz musicians who have played with the best, metal bands who could give Ozzy a run for his money, calypso bands, junkanoos, and opera singers. Key West even has its own symphony and is the home of Shrimp Boat Sound Recording Studio, which has hosted greats from the Smashing Pumpkins and Beach Boys to local hero Jimmy Buffett. If you are looking to dance, play the kazoo, or expose your hidden rock star at one of the karaoke bars, Key West is your place to feel the beat of the rhythm of the night. By the way we heard some crap the other night and it was pretty good.

Salt Please

In 1977, Margaritaville peaked at No. 8 on the pop charts and topped the Billboard charts at No. 1 in the "Adult Contemporary" category.

Festivals

Key West loves its festivals, but most people do not realize how they came about. There was a time when Key West had a little thing called tourist season. It dominated the typically cold months like January, February or March and people liked the money that came with the tourists. Months like August, September and October were very slow, but the locals needed money so they lured people down with festivals. The trick worked and new festivals were added each month. Pretty soon there were a lot of festivals and people figured if there was a festival for writers there should be a festival for pirates. Once the pirates had a festival, the bikers wanted one, then the boaters, then the lesbians, and soon the chickens. Before you knew it everybody had a festival. Today a good festival is just around the corner. We like to celebrate anything and everything including bike week, Hemingway Days, Conch Republic Days, holiday parades, Fourth of July festivities, Old Island Days, art fairs, street fairs, and even the wackiness of Jimmy Buffett's Parrot Heads in Paradise. That is just the tip of the iceberg. The festival to blow away all festivals takes place the last weekend in October. God bless Fantasy Fest. This is the festival where everybody and their cousin calls to crash on your couch and even floor space is at a premium. When the party ends we all celebrate our survival with a little festival.

Papa Knows Best

"The things that happened could only have happened during a fiesta. Everything became quite unreal finally and it seemed as though nothing could have any consequences. It seemed out of place to think of consequences during the fiesta."
~ Ernest Hemingway The Sun Also Rises

 **Attractions**

Walking down Duval Street, one can be attracted to the multitude of attractive people Key West attracts. Too much attraction can cause distractions so it is important to get out and move around, get the blood flowing and challenge our minds. We need to feel like we have accomplished something in our day besides the seven-story beer can pyramid we call Mount Weiser. We need… attractions. Key West is full of attractions that allow just enough education and enlightenment to convince others there is purpose in our lives while at the same time providing more entertainment than you can shake a stick at. Conch Trains, trolleys, ghost tours, treasure museums, the world's largest ball of lint, Writer's Houses (Chris and David's houses available for private tours to young attractive ladies) and historic house tours dot the island. Arm yourself with the arsenal of knowledge available from these attractions and then head down to sunset for an evening cocktail. You have earned it, and we hear they are working on an eight-story pyramid at the Schooner Wharf tonight. Sounds pretty attractive.

 **Carl the Crazy Conch Says:**

Key West's first attraction was the aquarium, built by the Works Project Administration between 1932 and 1934 in an effort to make Key West a tourist destination.

54 Tours

• •

We know tours are similar to attractions, but they were a part of David's life for years so tours get their own special page. In order to get the most out of paradise you really need to do some exploring. An afternoon at the library poring over old maps and journals may be some people's cup of tea, but most of us would prefer that someone else do the research and sift out the interesting facts for us to enjoy on a leisurely walk. Don't feel like walking? Hop on a plane, train or automobile and tour the island as John Candy would. Lucky for us Key West has no shortage of tours, and to be completely honest they are all excellent. If you have ever been to an historic city and forced to listen to a little old lady from the preservation society rattle off more dates than a calendar, you probably take to tours like a cat to water. Key West has a few things going for it that the preservation society did not. Take a rich city with a bizarre and colorful history, add in the ease of getting from point A to point Z, and then consider the zaniness of the local residents who will be providing your entertainment and you have one hell of a tour. Ghost tours, Conch Trains, snorkeling trips, lighthouses or museums are just a few of your choices. Take your pick and you are guaranteed to get a tour without the bore.

Whatever

"Same old slippers, same old rice, same old glimpse of paradise"
~ William James Lampton

55 Spring Break

Spring Break has taken on a different meaning for us in our late twenties and early thirties than it had when we were strapping young lads in college. It has always been an excuse to head to the beach, drink enough beer to render ourselves legally dead and watch the girls in bikinis. But back then we actually thought we had a chance of getting lucky with the ladies. Today we know better. Spring Break in Key West is not the fraternity and sorority alcohol-fueled invasion that you see in the movies because, quite frankly, it is expensive to stay, eat and drink here and the drinking age is 21. Cash-conscious students looking to get the most bang for their buck head to Mexico, leaving Key West with the well-to-do and their tag-along friends running up a booze bill on daddy's credit card. This does not mean we are exempt from honking scooter horns, wet T-shirt contests and more puddles of vomit on Duval Street than usual, but we just ignore these things, grab a seat on the porch at Bagatelle and think back to our younger days when we still thought we had a chance.

Chris Says:

"Speak for yourself, David. I still have a punchers chance and I'll go down swinging trying to grab me a couple more Spring Break chicks before I die, damn it! Who's coming with me?"
Editor's Note: Chris drank a little too much absinthe on the day this was written. He really likes to look at the Spring Break girls, but that's about all he gets.

56 Fantasy Fest

Living in paradise is no easy job. A pirate for the pirate festival, Santa at the Christmas parade, a rooster at Chicken Fest. By the end of the year it almost feels as though the silly costumes we wear are being dictated to us and if there is one thing the people of Key West will not stand for it is the bars closing before 4 a.m. That, and being told what to do. The logical solution is to host a party at the end of the year where everyone can dress how they want to, be who they want to be and act out their own fantasies in the streets of Key West. Fantasy Fest was started in 1979 during a time when tourism was but an infant in town and season lasted just a few months of the winter. The Keys were trying to attract more gay tourism, but the market was tough after a series of attacks on gays including Tennessee Williams. A group of Key West business men came up with the idea of an any-thing-goes street party to get the tourist season kicked off early and the first Fantasy Fest parade hit the streets complete with a naked Lady Godiva riding her horse down Duval Street. Twenty-five years have passed since that first parade, and like the Flintstones we are still having a gay old time.

Carl the Crazy Conch Says:

When getting body painted, it is good to remember that by the end of the night all of your paint will be rubbed off one way or another.

 **Organizations**

● ●

The people who come to Key West usually have a screw or two loose, but they are in good company. It adds to the funkiness of the island and inmates at the asylum think everyone else is the crazy one. Unfortunately the pleasures of paradise can prove to be more than some people can handle. They let a certain aspect of the island take control of their lives and before you know it, they are convinced there are CIA agents disguised as monkeys in the trees sending signals to the invading aliens with a telepathic agent secretly implanted in the local beer. This is the time for an intervention, but we don't want to spoil our own fun, so we turn to one of the many helpful organizations with trained professionals who are certified to handle such cases. Alcoholics Anonymous (we know who they are), Narcotics Anonymous, Suicide Prevention, Domestic Abuse Shelters, Red Cross, AIDS Help, the Homeless Coalition, AAA, Survivors of Shaved Ass Monkey Attacks. The island is blessed to have these groups on the island. They will talk you down from a bad acid trip, or jump your car when you break down. We'll be at the bar keeping an eye on your Bloody Mary.

Carl the Crazy Conch Says:

AA and AAA are right next to each other in the phone book. Both are designed to haul you off the curb.

58 Sea Life

Every time one of our girlfriends hits us with the "I just want to be friends," speech we go to our rooms for several days and have a good cry. Eventually a girlfriend who has not force fed our heart through the wheat grass press and started dating women comes by with a box of tissues and gives us the "more fish in the sea" speech. We take a walk and realize it is true. Key West has an abundance of sea life and you don't even have to go out on a boat to experience it. Pet a shark at the Key West Aquarium. Take a walk along the historic seaport and you can see tarpon over four feet long basking in the sun of the shallows. A flock of parrotfish can be lured from beneath the seawall of Mallory Square with a handful of bread crumbs, or if you don't have bread you can often fool them simply by spitting in the water. Even the gift shops on Duval are filled with treasures from the sea. Conch shells, sponges and every object you could possibly make from them be it a necklace, a lampshade or the famous sponge monster surround you. If you are looking to overload your senses, head to the reef for a snorkeling trip. Angel fish, rays, sergeant majors, and nurse sharks are included on the neverending list of creatures awaiting your arrival. Swim with them, feed them, and enjoy their beauty but make sure you don't get too close. They just want to be friends.

Special Ed

"Why does Sea World have a seafood restaurant?
I'm halfway through my fish burger and I realize,
oh my god, I could be eating a slow learner."
~ Lynda Montgomary

Bars

Have you ever noticed the bars in Key West? Not the ones in your jail cell, the ones that serve drinks. They take some looking around to find, but pick up a steady drinking habit like the rest of us and you will remember all their locations before long. It has been said that Key West has more bars per capita than anywhere else in the United States and that there is a church for every bar. Both of these statements were made by drunks to drunks, so the factual basis is nil, but it sounds good and makes for interesting conversation between beers. Key West is a drinking town, be that good, bad or indifferent, and a good part of our culture is based on activities that take place in the bars. The very first liquor license in Key West was issued to Pepe's, which once stood on the current location of Rick's on Duval. But the people of Key West don't feel they need a license to do much of anything whether it is drinking, driving or both. We have inside bars, outside bars, high-class bars, low-class bars, raucous bars, quiet bars, beach bars, Irish bars, Czech bars, gay bars, straight bars, clothed bars, naked bars, handle bars, monkey bars, candy bars and bars of soap. We need a drink after that one. Any suggestions?

Local Advice

Don't ask your service industry folks for drugs. We've said it before and we will say it again. They are not going to risk a felony so you can get high.

60 Restaurants

Two all beef patties, special sauce, lettuce, cheese, pickles, onions on a sesame seed bun. Say it in under three seconds and you could get a free burger, but be forewarned that if you are caught eating at a fast food restaurant in Key West we will stab you with a spork! Sure the Grimace is funny and we would all love a Taco Bell dog to call our own, but fast food is everywhere. Key West is a dining experience and though they may not ask if you would like to supersize your baked dolphin at Blue Heaven or allow you to order from a picture with a number on it at Mangoes, the value of your Value Meal is in the ambience, the atmosphere and the interaction with the locals who work in the restaurants. Treat yourself to breakfast at the bar of the Banana Café and then ask yourself the following questions: Could I order a crepe with a béchamel sauce this delicious at Burger King? Could I be waited on by a beautiful Swede named Carina at Wendy's? Even if Carina worked at a Taco Bell, would I be able to check out her butt with the cash register and the counter in the way? The answer to all of your questions is no, so get out of your fast food frame of mind, head down to Banana Café and check out Carina's butt. Order some food while you are at it or they will have you arrested for loitering. This is probably the best advice you will receive in Key West and what did it cost you? $9.95, please pull forward and pay at the next window.

Wine and Dine

More than 70 restaurants and close to 100 wineries participate in the Taste Of Key West every April, a popular fundraiser that raises more than $100,000 for AIDS Help.

Food

The first lesson on keeping up with the locals at the bars is never drink on an empty stomach. So before you dive head first into a bottle of Grey Goose, take a moment to enjoy the tongue-tingling treats that surround you. The celery stalk in your Bloody Mary ain't gonna cut it. Key West has been blessed with diverse culinary influences. Bahamian standards have melded with traditional Cuban cuisine plucking succulent treasures from surrounding waters to join them in creating an array of entrees best described as Key West fusion. Chefs from around the world have added their influences and the restaurants are bursting with food themes both tropical and traditional. Though the restaurants enjoy all the fame and glory, some of the best Conch cooking is prepared in the homes of our island's residents (If you're lucky enough to have Ann Marrero cook you dinner you'll know what we are talking about.) Fausto's Food Palace and the Waterfront Market are famous for their produce and the seafood is so fresh it will pinch your ass if you don't pay attention. These are also great places to find a date if you want to do some ass pinching of your own. Insert your own sexually charged produce jokes here. It's almost lunch time and we need a Bloody Mary!

Local Advice

Don't eat asparagus. It makes your pee smell funny.
Why is that anyway?

62 Cemeteries

The Key West Cemetery is a place everyone who lives here wants to go, we're just not in a big hurry to get there. That does not stop us from visiting our final resting place, because like other destinations in paradise, the cemetery is one of a kind. Built in 1847, the cemetery tract was ideal because of its central location and a higher elevation than most of the island. A limestone foundation makes digging to any great depth a challenge, so a majority of the graves are built above ground. Surrounded by a wrought iron fence, the cemetery is a serene and tropical place, loaded with palm trees, statues, poinciana trees and unique ephitats. "I told you I was sick," may be the most famous saying associated with a grave, but you will also find "devoted fan of Julio Iglesias," a midget named Abraham Lincoln and a grave that is gradually being engulfed by a fig tree.

There are other cemeteries in Key West such as the chicken graveyard at Blue Heaven, the cat burial grounds at the Hemingway House and a frog cemetery on Thompson Lane. Like the main cemetery, they are a huge draw in paradise and people are dying to get in.

For Whom the Bell Tolls

One of the city's early fire warning systems was a bell that hung high above the cemetery. The number of chimes alerted residents as to which neighborhood was burning.

Churches

● ●

We have always heard there is a church for every bar in Key West. These are the kinds of facts we love, so we decided to check it out, but the bar research has taken much longer than expected. Key West offers worship options for nearly every denomination, religion, faith and ideology with saviors ranging from Mohammed, Jehovah and Buddha to Jesus, God and Dial-a-Prayer. While the parishioners of some churches may be predominantly black, white, Cuban or gay, every church will welcome you with open arms. Many locals take advantage of this opportunity and attend a different church every Sunday for a year. The architecture and history of our churches is astounding as well. It's like styles from different parts of the world came here and were dropped in Old Town neighborhoods with reckless abandon. A properly planned Sunday stroll can take you past several churches and provides a great opportunity to hear choirs singing, church bells ringing and get a taste of the love and community spirit from the various congregations. After obsolving your sins, head out for a refreshing cocktail. We hear there is a bar for every church.

Forgive and Forget

"Mutual forgiveness of each vice, such are the gates of paradise."
~ William Blake

64 The Wharf

No James Bond movie would be complete without the meeting at the wharf. The silence of night is broken by fog horns in the distance and boats bobbing with the tide. Evil villains play poker in the cabin of a 50-foot schooner and a beautiful lady with a Swedish accent serves drinks at the bar while waiting to assist 007 in blowing everything to pieces. Welcome to the Historic Seaport of Key West, where Bond-style action takes place everyday. We may not blow things up, but the salty sea dogs, classic schooners and beautiful Swedish lady can all be found around this last little piece of old Key West.

Our favorite wharf is the Schooner Wharf. It is a great place to let your afternoon turn into an evening sitting at a bar stool, hanging with the locals and watching the unique mix of activity caused by the boats, booze, locals and tourists. Jimmy Buffett's recording studio, the Lazy Way shops, Turtle Kraals, Conch Republic Seafood Company and the water are only a stone's skip away, and the nautical surroundings will make you feel like an extra in "License To Kill." If you are feeling brave, ask the pretty blond with the Swedish accent for a martini. Shaken, not stirred.

Moore, Moore, Moore:

"License to Kill" was filmed in Key West. Some memorable scenes were taped at Harbor Lights and St. Mary Star of the Sea Church.

Treasure

Open the Key West treasure chest and you will not be disappointed with the booty, for this is one place where the cups runneth over with treasures of all shapes and sizes. Today is the day Professors Chris and David will talk treasure and keep you abreast of the finest gems across the globe. When it comes to finding buried treasure you can leave your metal detector in the closet with your sexuality and follow in the footsteps of Mel Fisher. Know your maps, round up some investors, buy a treasure hunting ship and keep a positive attitude. Mel brought fame to modern-day treasure hunting with his discovery of the Spanish galleon Nuestra Senora de Atocha, which wrecked off Key West in 1622, and the millions of dollars in gold that accompanied it. This allowed a lot of people to pursue their childhood dreams and made Key West one of the few places where "treasure hunter" is an acceptable job title. Check out the Mel Fisher museum while you're down here and see the history for yourself, you can even buy your own piece of treasure. Gold is not the only treasure in the Keys. There is a wealth of knowledge, an abundance of beauty and plenty of chests to make memories you will treasure for a life time.

Local Advice

When annoying locals with drunken screaming, don't say, "Hey man, it's Key West." We know it's Key West, that's why we live here and according to law #66758 you are allowed to throw beer bottles at anyone who yells this.

66 Scooters

Some people call them death machines, a lot of the island can't stand em, and even we wish they would self destruct if the horn is honked more than three times in an hour. Once you climb behind the handle bars and start cruising around the island, these so-called doomsday devices take on a whole new meaning. Getting around Key West is easy on a scooter. You can weave in and out of traffic, enjoy the breeze and get a tan at the same time. Parking is never an issue as the town has plenty of spots designated solely for mopeds, and there arc no meters on these spots, so feel free to give your quarters to the homeless. Don't have a scooter of your own? Head over to Pirate Scooter or any of the many places that rent them around town and get ready to rumble. An afternoon of enjoyment is just a flick of the wrist away, but with this flick you don't have to worry about someone walking in on you. People have said that scooters are a lot like sex with ugly people: They are both fun to ride, you just don't want anyone to see you doing it. This is not the case in Key West; scooters are a socially accepted mode of transportation and you can pull up next to a Harley or a hottie without feeling like a complete pansy idiot. Worried about looking silly in a helmet? Florida has no helmet law, thus ensuring you will look cooler than cool as you fly over the handle bars slamming head first into a palm tree. Live fast, die young and leave a pretty corpse.

Annoying commercial from when we were kids

"Scootin' high, scootin' low, scootin' everywhere you go. Scoot on by and say hello. Hi, hello, how ya doing. Scoot. We're going scooting now, everybody scooting now come on and go scooting with me!...CRASH BANG BOOM!"

67 Crazy Cars

You probably don't see too many crazy automobiles when you visit other parts of the country. Big cities don't need these four-wheeled whack jobs causing problems on their streets so they send them to an asylum at the bottom of Florida where they can receive proper treatment and plenty of meds. The streets of Key West are loaded with odd driving contraptions and we have become used to vehicles painted with the images of Jimi Hendrix or Bob Marley, covered in sod with an actual garden, or even topped with a big wooden egg encouraging you to eat it. There is a replica of the Titanic, small scale of course, cars with giant flamingos on them and a number of vehicles with shark fins protruding from their shell. Local artist Captain Outrageous has painted dozens of vehicles with a classic collage of island wit and artistry and there are several privately owned hearses. Looking for a crazy car experience of your own? Rent one of the odd-shaped electric cars, which can resemble anything from a mini Mercedes to an alien space pod and cruise the town in a car that is just as crazy as you. Don't forget to take your meds.

Aye Karumba!

Attempts have been made to reach Key West from Cuba in a 1951 Chevrolet pickup and a 1959 Buick. Both were converted to boats.

68 Walkability

Doctors recommend 20 minutes of cardio activity everyday. They also tell us to stop drinking and charge $95 for an office visit. It's a good thing Key West is a walking town or we would be in real trouble. The entire island is two miles wide and four miles long, and though few of us look forward to a four-mile walk, it is good to know we can check on our New Town friends if one of those bombs goes off that makes cars stop working. Most people spend their time in Old Town, which consists of only a couple of square miles. Nothing is more than 15 minutes away which means you could probably walk from the Gulf of Mexico to the Atlantic Ocean in half the time it takes Domino's to deliver a pizza if you are able to resist the temptation of all 96 establishments serving ice cold beers. Everything is in walking distance from the grocery store and laundromat to the restaurants, bars, beaches and bookstores. In addition to being good for your health, walking the island has some incredible social benefits. Stopping to chat with a friend on the corner, making a new friend on the way to the store, or happening upon a piece of good karma that never would have visited you in the car, happens all the time. We do find it strange that it always takes longer to walk home from the bar than it does to walk there, but it beats the hell out of traffic jams and those pesky DUI's. So let's grab a beer for the walk, drink to our health and hope we don't bump into our doctor on the way home. He wouldn't approve of our drinking and we still owe him 95 bucks.

Contain Yourself

Key West does have a open container policy but if you put your beverage in a plastic cup and behave yourself, the police usually turn a blind eye.

69 Fishing

If you have been fishing in the Keys, skip this page. You are already hooked and there is not a line in this section that would net the satisfaction of your own experience. If you have not yet been reeled into the Key West fishing world, read on. There is nothing like the exhilaration of a big red snapper on the end of your rod. The nibble, the tug, pretty soon you are hooked and the struggle for power begins. You may reel in a beauty or she could be the one that got away, but a bad day fishing is better than a good day shoveling snow. Snapper, tuna, dolphin and marlin all swim the offshore waters of the Keys with the nearby reef providing a never ending supply of fish for both food and sport. Finding a restaurant to cook your catch is never a problem or you can always catch and release so the fishies can hit the reef party that night and make more little fishies. If sitting around a bait bucket with your pole in your hands doesn't do it for you, realize that fishing in the Keys also includes some of the most beautiful waters in the world, getting a tan, cracking a few beers and getting away from the world of bills, cell phones, jobs, your spouse and anything else that gets on your nerves. Fishing is an excuse for just about anything. Missed an appointment? Sorry, I was fishing. Didn't make it to dinner? Sorry, I was fishing. Caught having an affair at the office? There is only so far the fishing excuse will go, but think of all the free time you will have after the divorce.

Food For Thought

Give a man a fish and he has food for a day; teach him to fish and you can get rid of him for the entire weekend.
~ Zenna Schaffer

70 Water Sports

● ●

If you are looking for a game of Marco Polo, head back to the kiddie pool. It will be more your speed and the water is warmer too. Key West watersports cover every adventure level from the relaxing to the extreme, but what would you expect from an island with water on every side? Floating would probably be the least adventurous water activity, but don't worry if you are out of practice. We have added salt to the water to assist with your buoyancy. Kite surfing and power boat racing fill the other end of the spectrum, with snorkeling, diving, kayaking, water skiing, wind surfing, sailing, tubing and parasailing filling in between. Just imagine your tanned body glistening in the sun as you cruise on a jet ski jumping over waves and getting saltwater splashed in your face while that special someone holds on to you for dear life as you cackle into the sunset. Beats the hell out of water polo, and everybody knows horses can't swim.

Horsing Around

A game of water polo consists of four periods each with seven minutes of actual play.

 **Reefs**

● ●

You probably realize by now that the reef has a variety of fish and sea life, but there are countless other benefits we reap from that big hunk of coral in the sea. Our coral reef is the only living reef in the United States and one of the largest in the world. If you want to see a nicer group of organisms clumped together, pack your bags for Australia, mate. The reef is protected and the damage caused by a boat running into her can take Mother Nature years to repair. Our forefathers were not so environmentally conscious and the wreckers used to intentionally lure ships onto the reef so they could reap the rewards. At one time, this made Key West the richest city per capita in the United States. A bike ride around the island will show you the other uses for coral. Walls around people's yards, decorative stones and even houses were once crafted from the reef, though this practice has been discontinued to help our flippered friends. The reef acts as a natural filter for our water and helps keep it clean so you can enjoy all of the blues and greens. It contributes to the ecosystem in ways we have yet to understand, and it provides a great place to check out pretty people in their bathing suits on the premise of watching fish. Snorkel trip, anyone?

Carl the Crazy Conch Says:

Coral reefs provide homes for more than 25% of all marine life - yet take up less than 1% of the ocean floor. The reef is bi-sexual, releasing both sperm and ovum every August, shortly after the full moon.

72 Lobster Season

From the moment drawn butter was introduced to the Keys, people have been looking for vehicles to deliver it from the table to their mouths. Oversized crayfish seemed ideal, so we dove in head first, picked the ocean clean and proceeded to ingest our daily requirement of lobster and oleo. Unfortunately, butter reproduces faster than lobsters, and supply was not keeping up with demand. To solve the problem, our friends at the Fish and Wildlife Conservation Commission designated a lobster season. Regular season runs August 6 - March 31, giving the little buggers approximately four months to relax without the fear of being boiled. Mini lobster season falls on the last successive Wednesday and Thursday of July and people come in droves. Lobster assassination kits fly off the shelves, lobster festivals close off the streets, the bars echo tales of mutant sea lobsters and you are hard pressed to have a conversation in which someone does not bring up their tickle stick. Finding someone to give you a lobster of your own is no great challenge. All you have to do is butter them up.

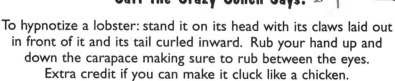

Carl the Crazy Conch Says:

To hypnotize a lobster: stand it on its head with its claws laid out in front of it and its tail curled inward. Rub your hand up and down the carapace making sure to rub between the eyes. Extra credit if you can make it cluck like a chicken.

 **Sailing**

Amazing waters, secluded islands offshore and a constant tropical breeze means get off your ass and sail the high seas. There is no better way to feel the joys of paradise than cruising by wind power through the water of the Keys. If you're not lucky enough to have a friend who sails, start drinking down at the wharf and befriend a sailor. Buy them a few drinks and ask them to tell you tales of the high sea. If that does not work there are several boats that will take you on sunset sails or even a night sail. The great thing about these boats is you don't have to do any work and they serve you all the free beer and champagne you can drink. We recommend going sailing in January. On your average sunny day, take a picture of yourself drunk during a beautiful sunset on one of those new-fangled camera phones and send it to your friends in Minnesota where its something like 54 below. They will hate you and nothing makes you feel better than knowing you're having a delicious afternoon sail in the tropics, relaxing with a beer while they are freezing their asses off trying to get home from work. The high seas of jealousy makes you feel like a champ.

 Rock the Boat

"Sailing is a good sport. You don't have to beat up the other guy like you do in boxing and football; you just try to outsmart him, and then you go out and have a beer with him."
~ John Kolius

74 Boat Races

● ●

Take two parts Jack Daniels, one part silicone breast implants, three parts red neck millionaires, add several million horsepower of screaming outboard motors and you have the Key West Power Boat Races. It is like NASCAR on the water, where everyone gets drunk and hits on their relatives while waiting for a crash. This is a great time to head for Duval Street and see some of the baddest boats money can buy. Most of the boats cost more than your house, unless of course you own a deteriorating one-bedroom in Old Town. Even the paint job on these boats can cost over $20,000. You want to ride in style when your average speed is close to 100 mph with a top speed of 200 mph! The powerboat races benefit us in many ways in addition to bringing money and excitement to the town. Boating technology as a whole has advanced because of the sport. Most of the personal pleasure boats used today achieved their hull and engine designs from information gained on the powerboat race courses, and most of the strippers achieved the breast augmentation designs from the boat racer's girlfriends.

Float Your Boat

Power boat racing can be traced back at least 100 years. The American Power Boat Association was founded in 1903.

75 Margaritaville

• •

Margaritaville is a song, a tequila, a restaurant and the subject of 129 trademarks starting with #78538851 in the United States Trademark and Patent Office. Being too lazy to review each of these 129 trademarks, we decided instead to risk our homes, livelihoods, financial security and anything else we could lose for trademark infringement to bring you, our dear reader, this section. (David and Chris – outlaw authors extraordinaire.) The term Margaritaville was created by none other than local legend Jimmy Buffett and though the lyrics to the song would fit well in just about any tropical paradise, those of us living in Key West are confident he was talking about us. Margaritaville, for us, is a state of mind that says, "Kick back on the front porch, chill out, have a beer and gaze mindlessly at the tropical surroundings. Anything that is a problem will have to wait until tomorrow because right now I'm enjoying my own little paradise." This is the mindset that keeps the locals living here and attitude that keeps the tourists coming down. There is something to be said for a place you don't feel guilty having a beer at 10 a.m., but no matter the time, you should go get a beer, so we can have a little word with Mr. Buffett. If your name is not Jimmy Buffett, skip the next paragraph and turn to the next page!

Hi Jimmy

We hope you are enjoying our book. We probably didn't even come close to capturing your meaning of Margaritaville, but to be quite honest we were a little lost after the whole spongecake line and people would have just skipped this section if it were called Chrisanddavidville. All of the other readers are on the next page now, so we will let you go. Can you write a song about us for your next album, maybe a bonus track on your next greatest hits? That would be cool.

76 Mystery

Isn't it appropriate that mystery pops up on the very page where you are wondering just what it was that we had to say to Jimmy Buffett? That is the great thing about mysteries – they keep you in suspense, and besides that, once they are solved they stop being a mystery and just become something else. Key West is full of mysteries and we are okay with that. Perhaps in a big city people would take the time to look into something long enough to find a meaning, cause or source, but here in Cayo Hueso we are quite content with the fact that at least one sock will be missing every time we empty the dryer. If you like your mystery served up on a spooky platter, Key West is pretty good for that too. People disappear without a trace, boats go down in the dead of night, and strange lights appear in the sky even when we are not hallucinating. We wonder about these things and talk about them, but that is about as far as we care to go. If you are looking to see a mystery solved, go watch Scooby Doo.

Local Advice

If you have an accent, please don't stiff your waiter.
It only makes them want to hurt you.

Bicycles

Bicycles are more than a two-wheeled form of self propulsion in Key West and you can tell a lot about a person by the bike they ride. From a rusted-out beach cruiser to a former rocking horse that has been fitted with wheels, you can find it in Key West. But before you go pedaling off into the sunset, there are a few things you should know. Bike thief is an occupation in Key West. You won't find it listed in the classifieds, but start smoking crack and you will discover the perks of this job once you have sold off all of your mother's jewelry. Lock your bike even if you are only planning to be a minute. This is Key West, distractions can happen and bikes have been known to disappear in less time than it takes to kick a pigeon. One of the greatest things about Key West is that you can get around anywhere with a bike. Everyone does it and it is the smoothest way to check out the island. There are bike paths on almost every street and convenient places to park near all of the bars. Be careful on that bicycle if you have been drinking. Did you know that you can be convicted of a DUI on your bike and lose the driver's license for your car? The cops are not out there conducting breathalyzer tests at the bike racks, but people have had this happen. More common is the person who rides the wrong way down a one-way street at night without a bike light. This is a clear sign to the cops that you are carrying crack, so even if you don't smoke crack, use a bike light at night and don't go the wrong way down a one-way street. Give your mom her jewelry back while you are at it, and stay off the tandem bikes unless you are gay.

Conch Connection

The planned Overseas Heritage Trail will combine old U.S.1 bridges with new bike paths to connect Key West with the mainland.

78 Southernmost Point

How could we call this paradise if we didn't have bragging rights on something? Minnesota has the biggest mall, South Dakota has the largest ball of twine, California has movie stars, think, Key West, think. Well, Hawaii is a little farther south than we are, but they are not connected to the United States and they didn't join until the end anyway, so let's call ourselves the Southernmost City. This is how it all began. Shortly after, the attorneys came in and added the small print about the continental United States and before you knew it we had the Southernmost Hotel, the Southernmost House, and the Southernmost Pool. It was only a matter of time before people started wondering where the Southernmost point of the Southernmost City was located, so a marker was created and a photo opportunity was born. The marker used to be located at the end of Duval Street but things started getting crowded so it was moved to the end of Whitehead. This is getting a little crowded too, but they could move it to Miami and it would not make a difference. The real Southernmost Point is on restricted Navy property, so no one can get there. The price we pay for paradise.

Southernmost Luck

It is rumored that if you are the first to rub the Southernmost Point buoy at sunrise you will be blessed with good fortune on your trip.

Off the Deep End

NO DIVING

NO
LIFEGUARD
ON DUTY
SWIM AT YOUR
OWN R.SK

photo: RobONeal.com

79 Small-Town Charm

Before we moved here we never really understood what small-town charm meant. Maybe that is because we always lived in big cities and were more accustomed to urban sprawl and sniffing glue. Small town charm is probably best defined as an intimate knowledge of the inner workings of a small society. It can be likened to farting on one side of town and having your friends call five minutes later from the other side of town to tell you what it smells like. Charming, right? This intimate knowledge has benefits besides knowing what your friend had for dinner. Knowing your neighbor by more than his first name, shortcuts and trails to ensure you get the most out of your wanderings, names to drop when resisting arrest and which bar to visit when you want a strong pour. We have a little something here called the coconut telegraph. Cell phones, e-mail and walkie-talkies could all take a flying plunge into the depths of Hell and we would still know that your husband is enjoying body shots at the local strip club when he says he is out fishing. Go easy on him. He is just enjoying the small-town charm.

 **Small Talk**

"The nice part about living in a small town is that when you don't know what you are doing, someone else does."

80 Dress Code

No shirt, no shoes, no problem. That seems to be the general attitude in Key West, but before you go skipping into Louie's Backyard showing off your beer belly and unkempt toenails to the world, realize that some restraint is in order. Most bars and restaurants don't give a hoot what you wear, so long as your naughty bits are covered and your money is not tucked away in an orifice. Some of the finer establishments prefer a clean shirt and some effort to look like you didn't just wake up in the gutter. You may have heard the phrase "Key West casual." This doesn't only apply to sex, but is a guideline for how to dress so you can get in just about anywhere. If you would wear it sailing you can wear it out on the town. Sounds like paradise, doesn't it?

Thinking of wearing a suit and tie? Get ready to field questions about the funeral, your court date, or the wedding. If you are going to a wedding, make sure to tell the single bridesmaids about us. We have a special dress code for our swimming pool we would like to show them.

Carl the Crazy Conch Says:

If I can wear a shell out for dinner, you will be fine with shorts and sandals. When I put my good shell on, I get a better table – if you catch my drift.

Tolerance

We don't just have a tolerance for alcohol, it applies to people too. Rodney King asked the question, "Can't we all just get along?" He was then brutally assaulted with a night stick. Here in Key West we learned from Mr. King not to ask such foolish questions and we decided a long time ago that we will get along. The booze goes a long way towards creating friendships and the pot helps us forget why we were angry in the first place. There is also such a bizarre mix of stereotypes down here that it would be hard to decide exactly which aspect of an individual you would choose to hate. Sure we get the occasional racist, bigot or homophobe in these parts, but it doesn't take long for these Archie Bunker types to realize they are the minority. We just laugh at the fact that they keep their homosexuality in the closet and pour another shot of tequila. Before you know it everyone has improved their tolerance.

Tolerance Defined

The capacity for or the practice of recognizing and respecting the beliefs or practices of others. Otherwise known as putting up with all the weird stuff people do.

Humor

If laughter is the best medicine, then Key West is a damn good place to get sick. The island has a great sense of humor, and unlike other places, we're not just laughing with you, we are laughing at you, too. If something is funny we are cracking a joke. If something is sad we are cracking a joke. If something is irritating we are cracking a joke, and every time we crack a joke we crack a beer to go with it.

Laughter is one of the keys that open the door to Key West. We find humor in the daily news, walking down the street, looking at chickens in the trees, watching drag queens break a heel and picking on German tourists in their black socks and Birkenstocks. Living as close to each other as we do, a good sense of humor is mandatory. The key to understanding this humor is in knowing that the people making the jokes are only distracting you from their own character flaws which, once discovered, will make for some great comedy. Don't take it personally, and if all else fails, make fun of the German tourists.

A Key West Joke

An accountant's dog, a gang member's dog and a Key West bartender's dog each get a pile of bones. The accountant's dog eats half of his bones and saves the other half for later. The gang member's dog beats up the accountant's dog, takes all of his bones and eats them. The Key West bartender's dog crushes his bones into a fine powder, snorts them, screws the other dogs in the butt and calls in sick for work the next day.

Diversity

● ●

Good afternoon, class. My name is Professor Slacker. Professor Shultz and Professor Sloan are hungover today so I will be your substitute teacher. Today's lesson is diversity, but quite frankly I find the subject boring so instead I am going to tell you about The Lance. The Lance is a man of mystery. He arrived in Key West in the late 1990s and let people know of his presence by writing his name on trash cans, boxes, newspaper machines and such. A common sample of his graffiti would read "The Lance is cool." The Lance then took to hanging around Duval Street with a sign indicating he would read out loud for food. And read out loud he has for many years. He only reads from one book, "Animal Farm" by George Orwell. One day The Lance had a sign that said "will read for money." The next day it said "will read loud for money." The third day he had a sign that said "will stop reading loud for money." Some people say his parents send him money to stay in Key West so he won't read in his hometown. Other people say he made tons of money in the dot-com boom and decided to come down here and read. Last time we saw him he was traveling down the street at about 22 miles per hour on an office chair. The Lance is cool. Very diverse.

Different Strokes

"If a man does not keep pace with his companions, perhaps it is because he hears a different drummer. Or maybe he's just a weirdo."

84 Opportunity

Since writing "Quit Your Job and Move to Key West" we have been approached countless times, not with invitations to sleep with beautiful women as you are probably thinking, but by smart ass know-it-alls who say, "Why don't you write a book that tells people how to get three jobs so they can afford to live here once they quit their jobs?" Our polite response is to comment on what a great idea that is and assure them that we will keep that brilliant idea in mind. But the truth is you don't have to work three jobs to live in Key West. It is an option many people choose, but there are always other options. Get ready, because we are going to let you in on a secret worth hundreds of times the price you paid for this book. Key West is the land of opportunity. It is a relatively small land mass that is visited by nearly three million people a year making it pretty simple to get yourself or your product in front of a good percentage of these three million people. It is not difficult to do, just pry yourself away from that Bloody Mary long enough to follow through on an original idea and you will meet with success. If you can't come up with an original idea, steal one from someone else – it seems to be all the rage these days. Believe in yourself and the community will believe in you. Shoot for the sky or shoot for the Skyy vodka. The choice is yours.

Lucky Charms

"Many an opportunity is lost because a man is out chasing leprechauns."
~ Drunk guy we met on St. Patrick's Day

85 Uniqueness

Do you know how to catch a unique rabbit? You neek up on it. Do you know how you catch a tame rabbit? The tame way, you neek up on it. We would like to apologize for subjecting you to this juvenile joke, but we have been looking for the right opportunity to repeat it since it was first told to us in third grade. This seemed like the right time, but based on your reaction it was not. Too bad, you are stuck with it now. With the onset of a global economy, uniqueness is rapidly becoming a thing of the past. Most big cities and suburbs with Wal-marts are the first to experience the cookie-cutter effects of a global economy. Luckily, Key West has been able to maintain a high degree of individuality and continues to offer many products and services that are one of a kind. Purple Baby Daddies, The Wave, Lloyd's Bike Tour, Looney Bin Creations. There is something to be said when the décor of your house is not easily identified as Pier One or Target. Your friends will gaze with wild wonder when they hear that you have a Key West original, they may even be briefly stunned. This would be a good time to hit them with the rabbit joke and get it off your chest.

Carl the Crazy Conch Says:

Rascally rabbits love to read Chris and David's books because they always have hoppy endings!

86 Friendships

If friendships came from McDonald's the ones in Key West would be supersized. Though that may be the most ridiculous statement ever printed in a book that was not written by Dr. Phil, it is true. Key West has mastered the meaning of friendship and taken it to a whole new level. We have best friends, good friends, close friends, drinking buddies, girl friends, guy friends and all of the friend types people have in other cities, but it goes far beyond that. We have friends we are only nice to when they have drugs and they are fine with that. Every gay person has a token straight friend. We have friends whose names we will never know, and they will never know ours. We even have friends we pass every day on the street but have never spoken to who would help us out in a pinch because, words aside, we have the common bond of passing each other at the same spot each day that has made us friends.

If anybody reading this wants a good idea for a television show they should pay close attention to the bonds that are formed in Key West. Call it "Friends" and you will have a supersized hit on your hands. No need to thank us – that's what friends are for.

 A Friend Indeed

When you are in jail, a good friend will be trying to bail you out. A best friend will be in the cell next to you saying, "Damn that was fun!"

87 Adventure

Set a course for adventure- your mind on a new romance. Key West is packed with more adventure than the Love Boat and Fantasy Island combined, but don't expect a midget in a white suit to greet you at the airport. Key West has a history of adventure going back to the days of pirates on the high seas, wreckers making their living from sinking ships, treasure hunters diving for lost gold and goodies and drug runners speeding away with the big score. Even today we have Cuban refugees landing on shore, hurricane evacuations and planes disappearing in our section of the Bermuda Triangle. The real adventure is waiting for you every time you walk out the door. It is not all that uncommon for a trip to Fausto's grocery store to get a simple loaf of rye bread to turn into an afternoon snorkeling off a boat with some people from Georgia then dancing the night away at Sloppy Joe's. The next thing you know you're waking up naked at the Southernmost Point using a loaf of bread as a pillow. The sense of adventure almost always outweighs the headache, or as Tattoo would say, "The pain, the pain."

Carl the Crazy Conch Says:

Six members from the cast of Gilligan's Island have guest starred on The Love Boat. The Professor is the only one who missed out on this adventure.

88 Local News

Your typical local news in Key West is a far cry from normal. While Miami news talks about murders, rapes and four-alarm fires, Key West is busy reporting on the new tiki bar being constructed at the wharf and the winner of the key lime pie bake-off. There are a few ways to get the local news in Key West. The Citizen, our local daily, has some decent articles and excellent columns by Mandy Bolen and Rob O'Neal, but most people pick it up for the bitching in The Citizen's Voice, a quick scan of the obits to see which neighbors passed on and the comedy of the Crime Report, where you can read about all the retarded things your friends did the night before. A typical crime report headline reads: "Drag queen arrested for beating sailor with a sex toy," or "Man arrested for fighting with neighbor's dog over turkey leg." If you feel like adding a face to the crime go to keysso.net and check out the mug shots. Words cannot express the feeling of satisfaction when you see the disheveled mug shot of a loved one and read all about their crime. Despite the benefits of the paper, the best way to get the news is to head down to the bar, pull up a stool and listen to the gossip flow. We'll take a drunken account of what really happened at the key lime pie contest over the Citizen's report any day. This is the place where the truth comes out.

Favorite Key West New Stories

1. Dog runs for mayor.
2. Silver man upset there is more than one silver man in town.
3. City hires nation's first chicken wrangler.

89 Coconut Telegraph

The coconut telegraph existed in Key West long before the Professor on Gilligan's Island started tapping out his useless SOS messages, but we like the Professor so we decided against taking him to court. The coconut telegraph is a system by which gossip disguised as news travels across the island via word of mouth faster than you could choose between Ginger and Mary Ann. We have always had a thing for Mrs. Howell and her coconuts, but let's keep that our little secret. When news happens in the Keys, word travels fast. This is great if you thrive on local gossip, but not so great if you are caught by your roommate in the midst of a romantic encounter with a mango. Many of these events don't make the paper, but even the stories that do are usually old news by the time they come out. We're going to have to cut this short. Just got word that Mr. Howell is in town and looking to kick our asses. Help yourself to anything in the fridge, we have plenty of fresh, ripe mangoes.

Through the Grape Vine

"Utility is when you have one telephone, luxury is when you have two telephones, opulence is when you have three telephones and paradise is when you have none!"
~ Doug Larse

90 Bubba System

The Bubba System is old school and you need to be a bubba to fully understand. You look like you are all right, so we'll let you in on how it works. Key West is a tightly knit community where people either know you, know of you, or can find out about you with a phone call or two. Nothing that happens on this island goes unnoticed so your island experience is largely determined by the way you behave yourself and the personal relationships you build. Friends of the cops don't get arrested; if you know the chef your dinner is free; Need a home loan? You should have thought about that before you had an affair with the bank president's wife. People who are giving of themselves in this community will not be alone when their back is against the wall, but if you do something shady, start looking for help in another town. Live here long enough and you'll get to know the benefits and pitfalls of it. We've got our bubbas and they've got us. Thanks, cuzzies.

Bubbalicious

The term bubba originated from the 19th century English term 'bub' meaning pal. The English derived this from the German word 'bube' which means apprentice or servant boy.

Funny Signs

Signs in modern society have become much too serious, and a little bossy in our humble opinion. Stop. Yield. No Parking. Pick up after Your Dog. This spot reserved for anybody but you. These are the signs of the times. Key West can always be counted on to add a funky little twist to things, so we have created a sign language of our own giving the middle finger to all of those other signs. "Speed Limit 14." "Please don't drop off chickens in the park." "Free beer tomorrow." "Beware of attack rooster." There is even a van with no doors that has a sign saying "locked." A church board during bike week read "God rides a Harley." A storefront promises "Inner peace through impulse purchasing." and even the cops have a sense of humor with their anti-drinking and driving campaign. "Drive hammered, get nailed." What does all of this mean? We have our needs and we need to post them, but a sense of humor goes a long way. We think that's a pretty good sign.

There's Always Tomorrow

The last day the Coral Isle Bar was open they crossed out the word tomorrow from their sign and it read "Free Beer Today!"

92 Self Expression

How often do we feel like saying something but stop short as our minds fill with doubt and fear? Too often. It is a reflex that has been etched in our minds since we stopped breast feeding, and an impulse that no 22-year-old should have to face. The only time we truly feel free to express our innermost thoughts without second guessing ourselves is in the company of close friends or in a friendly environment that encourages and nurtures this type of behavior. Self expression is alive and well and living in Key West. You can see it in our cars, our bars, our clothes and the silly books we write. Stumps are painted like an octopus, a Pontiac is made to look like the Titanic, a wall is made of bottles and a tree is covered with pre-chewed gum. Make your own bumper sticker, create your own T-shirt, write a poem or create a sculpture out of dog food. If riding your bike down the street in a clown costume carrying a bunch of balloons and singing Willie Nelson songs at the top of your lungs floats your boat, have at it. No one is going to stop you and most everybody will get a good laugh in before returning to their own adventure. That is what Key West is all about. It even lets goony writers pretend they are famous.

Material Girl

"Express yourself (You've got to make him) Express himself
Hey, hey, hey, hey.
So if you want it right now, make him show you how. Express
what he's got, oh baby ready or not! Express yourself!"
~ Madonna

Sounds

● ●

If you were to take a walk through Old Town with your eyes closed and a clothespin on your nose, you would probably bump into a pole and get a bloody nose. No one would want to help the blindfolded freak covered in blood with a clothes pin lodged in his nostril. You would bleed to death and your family would sue us for suggesting such an idiotic idea. None of us would enjoy paradise then, so let's just play make believe for now and you can have your imaginary lawyers talk to our imaginary lawyers. Enough of that. Key West is full of beautiful sounds that are yours for the taking if you sit back a moment and listen. Wind blowing through the palms, geckos chirping, cats fighting in the distance, roosters crowing, beer bottles clinking, cannons firing from the wharf, drag queens singing and neighbors having a good time. These are the noises that make the soundtrack of our island paradise. That and the sound of people laughing at the goofball with a clothespin lodged in his nostril.

Sound Advice

Quit trying to figure everything out. Sit back and listen!

94 Community Spirit

Did you ever notice that some people are proud to announce where they live, while others barely whisper it out, or in the case of New Jersey just lie and say they are from somewhere else? To the best of our knowledge, the only people who hesitate when announcing Key West residency are the mothers of men who live here who are afraid the ladies at the bridge club will think he is gay. Community spirit is a direct reflection of pride and who would not be proud to live, sleep, eat and breathe in the very place millions of people are scrimping and saving to visit each year? We live in paradise! We know it and we show it. We show it by supporting local causes, we show it by going to all of the high school, elementary and community college events and we show it by throwing a parade, party, festival or fundraiser every time someone gets a "C" on their report card or stubs their toe. Think of us as the dysfunctional family that sings their daughter's praises to the town because she didn't get knocked up until she was almost 16. We care about our community and we care about the people who live in it and visit it. This can lead to some heated, passionate arguments, but then again, so can one too many daiquiris. So, moms, be proud of your sons who live in the Keys! We are sure the lesbians at your bridge parties will understand.

Warning Signs That Your Son Might Be Gay

1. More than one Abba record in his collection.
2. The magazines under his bed have pictures of naked guys.
3. He is always giving you decorating tips.
4. He likes to rollerblade.

Attitude

A wise man once said, "Changes in latitudes, changes in attitudes, nothing remains quite the same." His name was Jimmy Buffett, still is, and you would be wise to listen to his wisdom. There is a theory that the attitude we apply to a given situation is in direct proportion to the brain's proximity to the Equator, hence the attitude of someone in Key West would be significantly more laid back than that of a person living in Vermont, unless the person in Vermont has a really large head. Look around Key West and you can see our laid-back attitude is everywhere. This is not to say we don't give a damn, we just don't get ourselves worked up if our food takes longer than expected, if a fishing trip gets rained out, or if our girlfriends start dating women. We came to realize a long time ago that a good attitude is all you need to rise up and walk away from a situation that is not going your way, and there is not a single problem that can't be solved with an ice cold beer at the Green Parrot.

Attitude Adjustment

"Changes in latitudes, changes in attitudes, nothing remains quite the same. Through all of the islands and all of the highlands if we couldn't laugh we would all go insane."
~ Jimmy Buffett.

96 Local Radio

● ●

Local radio in Key West is lacking at times, but like our ex-girl-friends, it is their personality that keeps us coming back for more. There are several morning shows with DJs who provide commentary and fodder about life in the Keys. You have your lesbians on the pop rock station, your drunken, arrogant funny man on the classic rock station, and an array of hip, laugh-at-their-own-jokes DJs on the alternative station. (Chris is a DJ here and laughs at himself all the time.) Each one brings the good with the bad, but it is quite amusing to bounce around all three stations and get their opinions about what is going down in the Keys. We are told there are other radio stations in the Keys that feature adult contemporary and country, but we only write about what we know, hence the frequent references to booze, sex and John Travolta. Hoebee, Vinnie K and Casey, Rude Girl & Molly Blue are the Howard Sterns and Casey Casums of Paradise and we would not have it any other way.

Socialist Distortion

Radio transmissions from Key West can be picked up in Cuba, keeping Castro updated on America's Top 40!

Smells

Put on a blindfold, plug your ears, open your nose and get ready for a great Key West experience. Gotcha we just farted! HaHa! Potty humor aside, Key West has such amazing aromas even Toucan Sam couldn't keep up with them, and all you have to do to experience them is take a walk down any street in Old Town. Check the garbage schedule before you head out and your nose will be graced with the sweet smell of frangipanis, citrus trees, mangoes, avocados and jasmine as well as the unofficial herb of Key West which always seems to be in bloom. We don't know where to get it, so don't ask. As you approach Duval Street the scents from the restaurants permeate the air and the ocean breezes mix in the smells of salt air, suntan lotion and Cuban cooking that will excite even the most discerning palates. There seem to be a lot of people in the Keys who like sniffing rolled-up dollar bills, but we have never been that attached to money so we don't quite get that one. We'll leave that to the fruit loops as we count our lucky charms.

Bars That the Cereal Cartoon Characters Would Visit if They Came to Key West

Cap'n Crunch – Schooner Wharf
Tony the Tiger – Bourbon Street
Boo Berry, Franken Berry and Count Chocula – Captain Tony's
Sugar Bear – La-Te-Da
Wilford Grimley – Grand Vin

98 The Dark Side

The great thing about sins is that God will forgive them, at least that's what our priest told us and he was a pretty good guy apart from the whole altar boy incident. If you are going to call a place paradise it has to cater to the desires of the majority, and unless the drug dealers and strippers are a bunch of trust fund babies, it is a pretty safe bet that the demand for the supply is out there. Smuggling, prostitution, drugs, gambling, sex parties and strip clubs all exist in Key West, but in keeping with everyone's ideal of paradise they are not forced on you or thrown in your face. If you are looking for a little pot, you will figure out where to find it, if you want to see naked women or men you can head to a local strip club. You don't need to worry about someone coming up and sticking a joint in your mouth or showing you their privates and forcing you to put a dollar in their g-string. This is your paradise and the choice between the apple and the mango is yours alone.

Night Visions

"Beware of the Dark Side.
Easily they flow, quick to join you in a fight."
~ Yoda

"Ain't nothin' gonna save you from a love that's blind
when you slip to the dark side and cross that line."
~ John Cafferty and the Beaver Brown Band
(also known as Eddie and the Cruisers!)

99. The Citizen's Voice

You would think living in paradise eliminates any reason to complain, and though it does for most of us, some people managed to sneak past the Miserable People Police (MPP) stationed at the Cow Key Channel Bridge and have found their place to vent in the Citizen's Voice. Roosters keeping you awake at night? Call the voice. Car got a flat? Blame construction and call the voice. Panties in a bunch? Blame everyone but yourself and call the voice. This anonymous bitch-fest has actually been taken to a new level and there are a number of locals who call in ridiculous complaints just to see if they will be printed. The more ridiculous your quote, the more points you score. Check it out for yourself each day on page 2 of the Key West Citizen. Having trouble finding the local paper? Call the voice and complain. Two points if you can work the word "balls" into your quote. The Voice can be reached at (305) 294-5800.

Let Freedom Ring:

"Free speech, exercised both individually and through a free press, is a necessity in any country where people are themselves free."
Theodore Roosevelt, 1918

100 Nicknames

● ●

Cayo Hucso, The Rock, Bone Island, The Conch Republic; Key West has a lot of nicknames and so, you will find, does everything and everyone who has been here long enough. Stick around and you will get one too. Nicknames usually consist of your first name combined with something about you such as your job or any odd feature of your appearance. If your name is Brad and you have a large mole on your forehead you will become "Moley Brad," or if you dance at a strip joint and your real name is Paula you will be "Stripper Paula." There is nothing mean-spirited about it because after awhile people just know you from the mark you leave or the marks you have. David owned the Ghost Tour so he is known as "Spooky Dave." Chris has really white hair and it looks as if he's never seen the sun so he has been deemed "Snowball." Hold your "Clerks" jokes with Chris or your nickname will be "Hospital Bill." Nicknames in town are cool, and we are not just saying that because it rhymes with Rick James. They are a term of endearment and a right of passage that help your fellow Key Westers make the most of their short-term memory loss. Just ask Nick, he's the guy who came up with the whole idea.

What's in a Name:

Key West has had such nicknames as Thompson's Island, Cayo Hueso, Key Weird, Gay West, Bone Island and The Rock.

 **Legends**

• •

Tired of living in a town where the only legends are located on the bottom right corner of a map? It is time for a different type of key, and Key West is the place where the legends are so great they are, um, legendary. Skunk apes lurking in the mangroves, things that go bump in the night, possessed dolls, hanging trees, hidden treasures, secret passages, Santeria spells, superstitions, traditions, wreckers and leaves falling from trees. Legends usually come in the form of first-hand accounts of incredible events that have been passed down through the generations by word of mouth. Most of them are based on some element of fact while others are grossly exaggerated, manipulated or just plain unbelievable. Key West has its share of each, but what would you expect from an island packed to the gills with history, adventure and more booze hounds than the St. Patrick's Day parade? Wondering about the leaves? Legends of the Fall. Ha!

Local Advice:

Never try to keep up with the locals. Remember, they drink all year and are not amateurs at pounding a load of drinks and getting up in the morning to go fishing. Watch yourself and you'll have a better time. We always recommend drink, drink water. Drink, drink water. It keeps you buzzed but out of the gutter. You'll thank us the next day.

photo: RobONeal.com

photo: RobONeal.com

 **You!**

● ●

Our publisher is not happy about this page.

"You can't have 102 reasons in a book called Key West 101!" One of the beautiful things about paradise is you always get a little more than expected. Better still, the final ingredient in paradise is you.

Paradise is not the elusive mystery people have made it out to be. There are no riddles to solve or secret codes to unlock and you don't need to recruit Charlie's Angels or bribe anyone with Scooby snacks. Paradise is everywhere, but you are not going to see it if you don't open your eyes.

When half of your last bottle of beer is gone you have two choices; complain that you are almost out of beer, or enjoy every sip of fine malt and barley like it was your last. Even when the beer is gone you can choose to admire the beads of sweat on the bottle or bitch to the other bar patrons about the raw deal life has handed you. Paradise is not a destination, but a journey, and your attitude will determine just how far down the road you travel. Paradise exists everywhere, but most people agree that it is easier to come by in the tropics. Our goal with this book is not to hand you paradise on a platter, but to provide you with some appetizers and enough ingredients to get you cooking on your own. We hope you learned a little and laughed a lot. If that is the case, our job is done. The island awaits you. It is time to discover paradise.

About David Sloan

David Sloan disappeared in 2003 under mysterious circumstances. A person claiming to be David returned in 2005, but certain things do not add up. If you encounter the fake David, do not approach him, for he may be armed. Please send any information regarding the real David to info@phantompress.com.

About Chris Shultz

Christopher Shultz lives and works in Key West. He likes eggs benedict on Sundays and enjoys talking on his banana phone. If you see him, say hello.

Also available from Phantom Press
www.phantompress.com

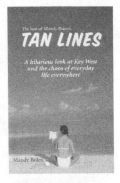

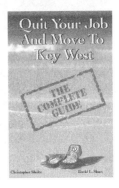